Roy Ullyett.

WHILE THERE'S STILL LEAD
IN MY PENCIL

His own story of more than 60 years
drawing a wage in Fleet Street,
with Norman Giller

ANDRE DEUTSCH

First published in Great Britain in 1998 by André Deutsch
76 Dean Street, London W1V 5HA
www.vci.co.uk

André Deutsch Ltd is a VCI plc company

British Library Cataloguing in Publication Data
A catalogue record for this book is available
from the British Library

ISBN 0233 99421 1

Printed and bound in the UK by
Butler & Tanner Ltd, Frome and London

For Maggie.
Thank you for the best years
of my life, so far. There
are still lots of lilacs
to be gathered.

Also for Freya, John,
Kate and Ben,
with much love
and affection.

*The photographs that appear in this book
are by kind permission of the* Express,
*and are also from Roy Ullyett's
private collection.*

CONTENTS

From the Bottom of My Bottom

AN APPRECIATION OF A CARTOONING GENIUS
By Lord (Colin) Cowdrey

R OY ULLYETT appears to have been around for a life time. Indeed he has, because the sixty-three years he spent as a newspaper sports cartoonist is possibly the longest career of any Fleet Street scribbler. I have the satisfaction of being one of the few of Roy's 'victims' who actually got an apology from him for the punishment handed out by his pen. When, during my days as Kent and England skipper, I protested about his treatment of my posterior – for making it of hippopotamus proportions – he produced the masterpiece below, which beautifully captures the genius of the man. It gave a whole new meaning to having a pen friend!

While on a cricketing assignment at a south coast resort, I found a saucy seaside postcard which featured the enormous bottom of a lady on the beach. I

sent it to Roy with the message, 'I did not know that your work appeared here too! It is obviously how you practice drawing my rear end.'

Let me briefly tell you the story of Roy's obsession with my bottom. Some forty-eight years ago one good innings in a vital Melbourne Test match set me on the road as an England cricketer. Alas, any pride at this personal achievement was dashed in a trice by the handiwork of Ullyett, translating the fourteen stone (and admittedly tubbier than average) England hopeful into something akin to the modern drug-produced Olympic shot-putting twenty stoner, with an enormous backside and innumerable double chins.

Such was the distortion that for years in the street I noticed people stop in their tracks, look me up and down and, after a quick glance at my posterior, remark to their companion, 'I thought that was Colin Cowdrey for a moment, but he is much too slim, young and good looking!'

The day I was joined in the England team by the larger-than-life Colin Milburn, Roy was in his element. You will find in one of the following chapters how Roy gleefully portrayed the pair of us. He managed to have us blocking out the sun, and making the ground tremble when we ran singles. It was hilarious, even for Olly and I on the receiving end of his unique and very heavy humour!

Despite all his haunting taunting of my weight, I have always been a devoted fan of Roy's and this book is a long overdue look back at his remarkable life and times. It tells the story of a sporting and journalistic world that no longer exists, and is like something out of an Evelyn Waugh novel. There are also fascinating glimpses of the show business world in which Roy has always dabbled. His original cartoons have become collectors' items, and over several decades he has raised many thousands of pounds for charities with auctions of his work.

Roy, famous for his enormous ginger handlebar moustache and the sparrow that always popped up as his cartoon companion, was dragged kicking and screaming into retirement in the spring of 1997 after forty-four years entertaining *Daily Express* readers with his brilliant cartoons that provided back-page fun in a sports world that has become increasingly competitive and serious. His magic touch brought much-needed light relief. Rather than hang up his pen, he went straight back to work compiling this book.

I am delighted that Roy has still got lead in his pencil, and I thank him for all the laughs he has given us ... from the bottom of my bottom.

Read and enjoy. There will never be another like him.

LORD COWDREY OF TONBRIDGE

Arthur! Arthur!

THIS IS ME, FOLKS, AND THIS
IS AN INTRODUCTION, JUST TO
GET THE LEAD FLOWING
READY FOR MY LIFE STORY.
AND, MY LIFE, WHAT A STORY!

It has been quite a funny life, so far.

As I look back through cartoonist's eyes on my eighty-four years on this mortal coil I can think of few souls lucky enough to have had more laughs than me, and, more important and rewarding, able to share the fun with so many people. I have mixed with kings, princes and quite a few queens, several yet to come out of the closet, and I have been within drawing arm's length of many of the most glittering sports and showbusiness stars of the century.

During the Second World War I managed to serve in both the Army and the RAF, and when I became a fighter pilot my American flying instructor told me: 'It will be interesting to see if you manage to kill any Krauts before you kill yourself.' I have been to Buckingham Palace to receive an OBE, met General Franco just before the Spanish Civil War, and have been pleasantly assaulted by the Crazy Gang, jokingly insulted by Muhammad Ali and have been mischievously passed off as an Archbishop's son and a Lord of the realm.

My pencil has taken me around the world, and when I signed with the *Daily Express* in 1953, following a tug-of-war with the *Daily Mirror*, the formidable proprietor Lord Beaverbrook told me with what proved total accuracy: 'You will not become a millionaire working for me – but you will live like one!'

Yes, it's been quite a funny life, so far.

Now, while there's still lead in my pencil, I want to share my memories before I leave the stage (hopefully, after I have received my telegram from the Queen and been involved in some great sex scandal – a little joke that will get me an ear-bashing from darling Maggie, my wife for fifty-odd, very odd, years and the only real love of my life).

I earned my daily bread as a Fleet Street sports cartoonist for more than sixty years, but have always considered myself part of the show business entertainment world. My earliest cartooning days were spent at the music-hall, capturing the great artistes with my pen and ink. I never got that magical world out of my system, and I have stayed very much in touch with show business as a Companion member of the Grand Order of Water Rats for more than forty years, the last ten

3

as, proudly, one of only twenty Companions, along with the Duke of Edinburgh and the Prince of Wales.

It is the sports world with which I am most closely identified, and in the following pages I present the story of seven decades of British sport as witnessed by me in a privileged quick-on-the-draw capacity. It is a sporting history bounding on hysteria. But before we go off on a cartoon journey through sixty years of sport, with occasional diversions into show business, I invite you to come with me back to my early days. I need to give you a quick sketch of my background so that you know what compelled me to spend a life time in the search of the funny face of sport.

I want to take this opportunity to thank my old Fleet Street chum Norman Giller for helping to keep my rusting memory oiled. He first suggested this book some thirty years ago when we were earning our daily bread with the *Express*. What a good idea, I thought, and here we are sprinting into print. Sorry it took so long, Normie, but I've been rather busy.

My thanks, too, to André Deutsch Managing Director Tim Forrester for encouraging me to draw on my experiences for this book, and to Louise Dixon for her editing skills. I am also grateful, of course, to Lord Colin Cowdrey for the kind words in his introduction, and I make belated apologies for the way I portrayed his posterior. Put it down to posterity, Colin. I also acknowledge Richard Addis, Editor of the *Express*, where I spent the best years of my life, for his permission to re-publish many of my cartoons. I hope they are still funny.

Most of all, my thanks go to my daughter Freya for being there, and my wonderful wife Maggie for putting up with me for all these years. She deserves a medal. I shall draw her one first thing tomorrow.

I recall that when the Crazy Gang ever had a first night of one of their new shows at the Victoria Palace, their chief clown – my dear old pal Bud Flanagan – used to give me instructions. He would tell me to start calling for the author from my seat in the stalls the moment the final curtain came down. His actual orders were, 'Call Arthur, Arthur.'

Now here I am, an author in my own write. I hope I can convey just some of the marvellous fun that I have had ... while there's still lead in my pencil. Arthur! Arthur!

Yes, it's been quite a funny life, so far.

Roy Ullyett

WESTCLIFF-ON-SEA, ESSEX
SPRING 1998

1: Before I leave the Stage

HOW, WHERE AND WHEN I
STARTED OUT AND LOTS OF
EARLY-DAYS PERSONAL STUFF
THAT JUST MIGHT BORE YOU TO
TEARS. I WOULD SKIP TO THE
NEXT CHAPTER IF I WERE YOU.

I FIRST drew breath (ouch!) in Leytonstone in the first year of the 1914-18 war. I only wish that to hold your attention and, for the sake of a good read, I could paint a portrait of a poor, hungry artist chalking on the pavement to earn a crust. Sorry, but the picture is the opposite. I was born into comfortable surroundings in what was then a fairly posh quarter of the far side of East London on the edge of the Essex countryside. My father, Henry John Emerson Ullyett, was the manager and secretary of the fledgling sports manufacturing company, Slazengers.

We lived, my father, mother, two older brothers and I, in a grand, rambling Victorian house with a neatly manicured garden and an orchard in the grounds. When I returned to Leytonstone a few years ago to see if the old house had stood up better than me to the march of time I found it had been demolished to make way for a builder's yard. Oh well, at least I am still standing. Just. But I am aware that the demolition squad could arrive at any time.

This is the first time that I have been old, and it is most peculiar. I struggle to remember what I had for breakfast this morning, yet I can recall events of fifty, sixty and even seventy years ago as clearly as if they happened yesterday. And you know what a lousy day yesterday was. My fear is that chuntering on about my early days could drive you to the depths of boredom, but a sketch of my early life is necessary if I am to give an overall picture of how I managed to draw a wage as a cartoonist for more than sixty years.

I do not have to dig too far back into my family history to find an ancestor with an eye for art. My great-grandfather Glover on my mother's side was a noted Victorian artist whose oil paintings of Essex landscapes show a fine eye for detail and composition. The Glovers were a family of nineteenth-century London carriage makers and coach builders, before the emergence of the infernal motorcar.

It was music that occupied my father's side of the family. My paternal grandfather was an enthusiastic composer and conductor, particularly of choirs. On the mantelpiece at my home I have a beautiful chiming clock made out of red tortoise shell and ornamental brass. It was presented to Grandpa Ullyett by the Leytonstone Choral Society in 1878 for his work with them, and somewhere in Folkestone there is a plaque acknowledging similar baton-waving service. I would much rather the clock than the plaque. A plaque does not keep very good time.

My father was a capable water colour artist, who made a speciality of painting horses. But, like his father, his first love was music and he was able to play just about any wind instrument, while I only got as far as conquering the ukelele. What he passed on to me was an insatiable love of the music-hall, and all my best childhood memories are of visits to the theatres of the day to watch the finest entertainers performing on stage. Had my father had his way he would have been up there on stage rather than watching from the stalls. He was a fine singer, and I grew up surrounded by the sound of old music-hall songs. If he had told his parents that he was off to Cairo to run a brothel they would have told him they were not pleased but, thank heaven, he did not want to go on the stage.

I knew as early as six or seven that I had a sense of humour above the norm. The proof came during a visit to the Palace Theatre in Westcliff-on-Sea, Essex, to where we moved from Leytonstone and where I have had my home for most of my life. Master of comedy Stanley Lupino was topping the bill, but it was a down-the-bill double act that made a lasting impression on me. One of the characters was continually banging a stick on the stage, chanting in Chico Marx style: 'I make-a da music.' This creased me up so much that I fell off my seat laughing and I somehow got wedged in the adjoining seat, which of course made me laugh all the more as my mother and father tried to extricate me. It stopped the show, and I make-a dem all laugh. I must have enjoyed the moment because the memory has stayed clear with me for nearly eighty years!

The seaside home in which I grew up was strictly Victorian in discipline and outlook. My father kept a collection of whippy canes in a stand in the hallway, and was quick to put them to cutting use around our calves and backsides if any of we boys broke a strict code of conduct. Mother was a cheerful soul who hated seeing any of her sons whacked, but these were days when discipline was beaten in to you. I had selfish reasons for being anti-corporal punishment then, but when I see the behaviour of some of today's youngsters I feel a quick crack from my father's cane would be just the thing to teach them respect.

Come rain or shine, my father used to don his frock coat and silk top hat on board meeting days

Perhaps there was some violence in my father's blood. We believe that our main Ullyett ancestor was a Viking, who missed the longboat home after a few weeks of raping and pillaging. I have carried on where he left off, because I was always missing trains, buses, boats and planes. The raping and pillaging is yet to come.

Father was a keen cyclist, and encouraged us to keep fit through sport. He believed in a cold-shower start to the day followed by a brisk walk. Motorcars never played a part in his life, and he managed to retain his Victorian principles and values right the way through to the end of his life after the Second World War. On board meeting days he would go off to the Slazengers head office in London wearing a frock coat and top hat, but most days he just wore a plain suit. He would often come home with the latest line in tennis rackets and golf clubs, and with this sort of benefit I was able to play a mean game of tennis as a member of the Westcliff-on-Sea hardcourts club and I developed into a single handicapper at the great game of golf that has given me a lifetime of pleasure.

My formative years coincided with the 'Roaring Twenties', but the only roaring I can recall came from an uncle who had a yacht on the Norfolk Broads, where I used to spend lazy, hazy summer holidays. Uncle Billy used to turn purple with rage as he roared at passing boats on which gramophones were playing the latest hot dance numbers and piercing his peace and quiet. 'Throw that dratted thing overboard,' he would yell. 'The gramophone is the worst invention of all time.' I have become rather like that when somebody is sitting alongside me on a train sharing blaring Walkman music with me through their headphones. I find myself wanting to shout, 'Throw that dratted thing overboard!' Something I have learned from my visit to this planet is that everything changes, yet everything stays the same.

My two brothers and I carried on the family tradition of having three forenames. There was Basil Henry Ernest, who became a City businessman on the Royal Exchange; Norman William Kendall, who died of a fever at the age of twenty-three while working for the East India Bank in Madras; and then me, glorifying in the names Roydon Herbert Frederick.

The three of us were packed off to boarding school at Earls Colne Grammar in Halstead, Essex. It was a distinguished old school, founded in 1520 when Henry VIII was on the throne, and famous for its academic record. R.H.F. Ullyett, a real day-dreamer of a boy, did nothing to add to the scholarship glory of the school. We all wore straw boaters made in Luton that we traditionally used to throw out of the train window on our way home at the end of term. It was here at Earls Colne that I consciously became a scribbler. I doodled away many a lesson by drawing caricatures and portraits of my teachers and classmates rather than giving full attention to what was being said.

Some time in about 1927, when I was thirteen, the Government announced a cut in defence spending and that there was to be a drastic pruning of Army regulars. They knew, of course, that there could never be another war. I sketched my classmates as a squad of boy scouts and headlined it 'England's Last Line of

Defence'. The Editor of *The Colonian,* the school magazine, was sufficiently impressed to give it half a page. It was my first published cartoon.

A year or two later, one of my schoolmasters, L.K. Lucas, urged me to enter a national competition organised by British Fisheries who wanted to encourage people to eat more home-caught fish. I turned the map of Britain into a drawing of a fisherman, which hooked me the handsome first prize of a guinea. You could buy a lot of fish (and chips) with that. I later learned that L.K. Lucas also received a guinea for arranging my entry. It was my first experience of having an agent!

My drawing ability just came naturally to me, and I was hindered rather than helped by school art lessons in which the teacher spent hours instructing us to draw circles, cubes and all sorts of symmetrical shapes, pyramids and boxes. If I had paid too much attention to her – a Miss Pyke – she just might have suffocated at birth any talent that I had, because my style of drawing was frowned on by the purists and was considered frivolous. Contrary to that view, I consider cartooning a unique art form. If there is a lesson here for any budding young artist it is that you should by all means listen to the so-called experts, but develop your own style. Put *your* personality and interpretation into your paintings and drawings. Too often gifted young artists become the puppets of convention, and their natural gift disappears into a pit of predictability.

I was a straw-boatered schoolboy. This is how I was scribbling in the mid-1920s.

I like to think that my drawings are as personal and exclusive as a thumb print. It was once said of me by my former *Daily Express* Editor, the legendary Fleet Street master Arthur Christiansen, that 'there are thousands of people who draw but there is only one Roy Ullyett.' That meant a lot to me because I have always tried to be individual, and to take a stand-aside, distinctive view of events. If a picture paints a thousand words, then a cartoon should convey one thousand and one because it combines the image of what the eye sees with what the imagination adds. I developed my own distinctive style, but if I had an influence it was the exceptional, self-taught Victorian cartoonist Phil May. He was economical with his lines, and never fell into the trap of putting in too much detail. I have always believed in keeping it as simple as possible, concentrating on giving extra emphasis to the key lines to get the main thrust of the cartoon across as clearly and as quickly as possible. If there is any secret to cartooning it is be simplistic. The cardinal sin for any cartoonist is to confuse the reader. Above all, be observant. There is a whole cast of characters out there. Just use your eyes and make mental notes of their characteristics, and then jot them down on a sketchpad. Observe, keep it simple. Here endeth the art lesson. Now, back to school.

After my father had laid down the law about my school reports, I studied harder and managed to pass the Senior Cambridge exam. My unexpected examination success coincided with the world-wide recession that triggered the Wall Street Crash and generated the rise of Hitler and Nazism. Suddenly my father was financially stretched, and the chances of a university education went out of the window.

I left school in 1930 with the country in the grip of a crippling recession, and the unemployment queues were growing by the day. Father used his influence to get me an interview for a clerical job with the City of London. I had two sponsors, a high-powered City solicitor and the Lord Mayor elect. There was one job, six hundred applicants. I got down to a shortlist of ten, and we were all interviewed in turn by grandly robed City aldermen at the Guildhall. It came down to who you knew rather than what you knew, and the job went to the boy who had the current Lord Mayor as his sponsor. I was promised the next vacancy.

I then briefly landed a job with a commercial printers where there was a small art department developing poster and advertising campaign projects. The man in charge did not take kindly to the lanky, seventeen-year-old pipe-smoking new boy coming up with brighter ideas than him, and he quickly decided there was no place for me among his trainees who had all concentrated on that bit about symmetrical shapes and could draw conventional objects much better than me.

So, pipe clenched between teeth, I got on my bike – the only mode of transport I could afford – and set off looking for freelance work as a cartoonist. A pipe has been an essential accessory of mine from just a matter of weeks after I left school. I had caught the habit from my maternal grandfather, Ernest Glover, who turned pipe smoking into an art form. He had dozens of pipes of all shapes and sizes, and he used to carefully and expertly mix his own tobacco and keep it in a ceramic pot that now adorns a shelf in the study at my home. I have a vivid memory – both visual and nasal – of grandpa sitting in his armchair in his frockcoat puffing on his pipe and sending out an aroma that, to my young nostrils, was like the scent of heaven. I have since travelled the world surrounded by a cloud of tobacco smoke, and hope that somewhere along the way I have given people the same pleasure that I had getting a whiff of grandpa's fragrance. But these days pipe smokers are more likely to be treated like outcasts. How sad. With me, I'm afraid it's a case of love me, love my pipe.

Every birthday and Christmas my brothers and I used to pool our money and buy Grandpa Glover a new pipe. Grandpa, the quintessential English gentleman, would make a great show of packing it with tobacco that he first of all carefully rolled between his thumb and forefinger. Then he would hold a taper over the roaring log fire, and slowly light the pipe. We would watch him drawing on it with all the intensity and concentration of a *bon viveur* at a wine tasting, and after a couple of puffs he would always say through what was almost a halo of smoke: 'Magnificent. No man in this universe ever drew on a better pipe. You boys have made an old man very happy. Thank you, thank you.' It was possible to warm your hands on his praise. Years later, when the lovely old boy passed on, the drawers of his desk were found stuffed with our pipes, all still packed with the tobacco he had put in on the day he received them with such warmth. What a wonderful actor he was.

Grandpa Glover telling me that this was quite the best pipe he had ever smoked

My first approach to a newspaper in my new self-appointed role as a freelance cartoonist was to the local *Southend Standard*. The editor sniffily looked at my examples, and said, 'Sorry, but we've already got a cartoonist.' I nearly bit through the stem of my pipe as I cycled home.

Next stop was the weekly *Southend Times*. There had been the annual angling contest off the famous Southend Pier that week, and I had gone along with my sketchbook and captured the highlights. I showed the drawings to the editor, a buck-toothed Canadian, who seemed quite impressed. 'Hold on, sonny boy,' he said with a trans-Atlantic drawl while removing an ever-present cigarette that seemed glued to his bottom lip. 'We'll have to have a board meeting about this.'

He then opened the door leading down rickety stairs to the small printing room. 'We got any space for a drawing of anglers fishing off Southend Pier?' he shouted to the printer, who nodded his head to indicate there was indeed space for such a catch.

'How much can we pay for a full page?' the editor called to the man, who was clearly the senior director.

'No more than ten bob,' came back the reply.

That was the board meeting.

'Right,' the editor said to me, 'I'll pay you ten shillings, and please come back when you've got something similar to show me.'

My pipe was sending out joyous smoke signals as I swaggered out of the *Southend Times* office ten shillings richer and with what I considered an order for more work.

I looked around for inspiration and noticed that the local Palace Theatre was featuring *Rose Marie* by the Westcliff Operatic Society. With my new muscle as a pencil-carrying representative of the *Southend Times*, I called in to see the theatre manager and talked him into letting me meet each main member of the cast for a sketching session. They willingly took turns to pose for me. This was the big time, for them and for me.

I worked through the night composing a montage of the cast, aided by a batch of still photographs that I had borrowed from the theatre photographer. The next morning I proudly presented my work of art to the editor of the *Southend Times*, who nearly swallowed his cigarette when he saw what I was dropping on to his desk.

'Hold on, sonny boy,' he said. 'We'll need to have a board meeting about this.'

He shouted downstairs to the senior partner. 'We got any space for a drawing of the *Rose Marie* show?' The printer shook his head.

The editor looked at my face that had obviously become longer than a wet weekend in Ostend. He could see the trouble I had gone to with the montage, and boldly decided on a unilateral decision.

'Look, sonny boy,' he drawled. 'I'm going to do my best to find room for this and will pay you a ten bob fee that will just about break this week's budget. But please don't do any more work without us contacting you first.'

It was my first experience of, 'Don't you call us, we'll call you.' The pipe was giving out distress signals as I walked heavily out of his office.

Three days after the publication of the

The editor who launched my career at ten shillings a week.

Southend Times containing my montage I was summoned by the editor. 'Well, sonny boy,' he said, 'it seems like you've got a permanent assignment. We've had a board meeting and decided that we would like the sort of drawing you did on *Rose Marie* every week for a ten bob fee.'

It transpired that for the first time in the history of the *Southend Times* every single copy had been sold, and when the circulation manager – who was also the printer and boardroom consultant – made inquiries he discovered that the cast of *Rose Marie* had toured Southend buying up every copy.

The Palace Theatre ordered the original, and had it blown up to poster size and plastered the town with it as an advertisement for the show.

Roy Ullyett, the boy with the pen, the pipe and the pedals, was on his way.

I found a novel and titillating way to develop my drawing. While joining in swimming parties on Westcliff beach, I'd use small seashells to sketch faces on the sandy thighs of the local girls. I think a few boyfriends might have wanted to skin me. They obviously drew the wrong conclusions.

My income from the *Southend Times* was supplemented by a regular fee of one guinea for a cartoon in the technical magazine *Wireless Weekly*, which was bought by wireless buffs seeking inside information on how to put together crystal sets and to improve the reception.

I got the work on the recommendation of my brain-box cousin Kenneth Ullyett, who wrote technical articles for the magazine. He was such a whiz that he made a fortune out of the

'It's all right. He came up to the BBC studio by tube.'

An example of my work for Wireless Weekly. *The magazine was printed on art paper, and so I made it more of a painting than a drawing. I was 19 when I had this published.*

The Southend Operatic Company gave me early experience with the pen-brush and ink. This was typical of the weekly montage that I was having published in the Southend Times *when I was in my late teens and learning my craft. I would lightly sketch each subject in pencil, and then go over it in ink. My fee was ten shillings, plus the perk of free entry to the best shows in town.*

broadcasting revolution, and at one time owned a house in the grounds of Hampton Court and had in his garages seven vintage Bugatti motor racing cars. Me, I still had a bike and when I asked the editor of *Southend Times* for a rise was told, 'Don't you dare put a pistol to my head, sonny boy.'

I created a busybody character called Edgar for the *Southend Times*, and I also concentrated much of my work on spotlighting the local theatre productions. This was noticed by a friend of my father's, John Southern, who just happened to control a string of theatres including the London Pavilion, Victoria Palace, Garrick and the old Collins Music-hall. He suggested to the editor of the theatrical magazine, *The Era*, that he should take me on the staff. As Southern was his main advertiser, the editor was hardly likely to ignore the advice. Once again the old who-you-know-not-what-you-know factor had come in to play.

One of my first assignments for *The Era* in 1932 was to visit the Victoria Palace to draw the Crazy Gang. For any younger reader who may have stumbled on to this book, let me tell you that the Crazy Gang was a collection of oddball comedians who, I suppose, could be said to have laid the foundations for the Goons and, later, Monty Python. In fact Spike Milligan once told me that when the *Goon Show* idea was first put to the BBC, they wanted to call it *The Junior Crazy Gang*.

The original Crazy Gang were genuinely, almost certifiably crazy. Their unelected but unquestionable leader was Bud Flanagan, who was a walking, talking mirthquake. I remember Bud inviting me into his dressing-room where

he had agreed to 'sit' for a cartoon portrait. 'I want this to be a real close up of my beautiful face,' he said, moving ever closer to me while I was giving all my concentration to my sketchpad. Suddenly he reached out and snipped off my tie with a pair of scissors. The tie was worth considerably more than I was being paid for the cartoon, but it was a priceless moment in my life. I fell off the chair laughing, just as I had all those years earlier when watching the comedian make-a the music.

On another occasion, Bud invited me into the wings at the Victoria Palace. 'I want you to take careful note of this next double act,' he said. 'You will find something well worth drawing.'

They were a duo of quick-change artistes, who would take turns dashing off stage and rushing back on within seconds in a different costume. One of them came off for his third change, put his foot into a shoe and suddenly came to a dead halt. That

Flanagan and Allen, 1934

14

old rascal Bud had nailed the shoe to the floor. Years later, I drew a cartoon of Bud that was blown up to life size and hundreds of his fans queued to pose with it in return for a donation to the fantastically successful Leukaemia Fund charity he set up following the tragic death of his son.

I became close pals with Bud, whose real name was Chaim Weinthrop, and to this day I have not seen or heard a funnier comedian. You only had to look at his bulldog-in-a-bag face to laugh. It was the face that launched a thousand quips. He was a gift to cartoonists with his ankle-length, moth-eaten fur coat and battered old straw hat. His partner, Chesney Allen, was much quieter and the sanest member of the Gang. He was the perfect foil for Bud, whose madness knew no boundaries. To this day we are reminded of Bud's endearing quality when he is heard singing *Who D'You Think You're Kidding Mr Hitler* as the theme song to *Dad's Army*. In one of life's cruel twists, Bud also died from leukaemia.

You quickly learned to be on red alert when in the company of the Crazy Gang. It was commonplace for any one of them to pour the soup of the day into your briefcase, tie your shoelaces together or give your overcoat to a passing tramp. I was once on a sketching assignment in Bud's dressing-room when he was in deep discussion with a City gentleman who had called in with a business proposition. Bud held his attention while in the corner the manic 'Monsewer' Eddie Gray, who always talked tortured Franglais, was busy with the scissors. He carefully cut the businessman's bowler hat into layers, and then laid it back on the table, looking as if it was still in one piece. It was hilarious to watch the City man's face as he tried to pick up his hat in instalments.

Eddie Gray used to walk to and from the theatre trailing an empty dog lead. Time and again he had unsuspecting bystanders helping him look for the non-existent animal. I would say that he was in the Eric Morecambe/Tommy Cooper class for being a naturally funny man.

Monsewer Eddie Gray

Beneath a large strawberry of a nose he sported a false black handlebar moustache on which you could have hung a suit. When his son was born, I drew a picture of the baby with his dad's moustache. More than thirty years later, his son told me that he still had the drawing. I first started to sprout my tash in the mid-1930s. I was still in my early-20s and trying to make myself look older at a time when I was mixing with Britain's top entertainers. Eddie used to tell people that we were twins with different fathers. My trademark handlebar moustache has been with me for more than sixty years, and I suppose you could say that it has now grown accustomed to my face.

My very first cartooning appointment for *The Era* was with the then ninety-something Charles Corborn, famous for his 1890 song, *The Man Who Broke the Bank at Monte Carlo*. I sketched him backstage at the Garrick after he had given a remarkable final farewell performance. As he came off into the wings to thunderous applause he flopped into a chair and closed his eyes. His concertina breath was sounding like the death rattle. I was about to call for a doctor when he opened one eye, and said, 'And what can I do for you young man?'

I remember sitting in the front row of the stalls sketching the great variety theatre comedian Billy Bennett during one of his monologues. Suddenly I was aware of what seemed like raindrops hitting my sketchpad. It was spittle coming from Billy as he shouted his lines in true old music-hall style. I looked up and noticed to my great amusement that the conductor in the orchestra pit was covered in spit! That really make-a me laugh. Another time I was drinking in the bar of the London Pavilion with that grand old music-hall comedian Charles Austin, who specialised in portraying a cockney policeman called Parker. We were served by what would be described in those politically incorrect days as a barge-bum barmaid. As she ambled away, Charles nudged me. 'She fancies you, y'know,' he said, 'and she could crack walnuts with that arse of hers.'

He was a favourite of mine along with another exceptional character comedian, Will Hay, whose stage schoolmaster sketches made such a successful transition to the screen. Whenever I was with Will he wanted to talk about the stars – the twinkling kind. He was an expert astronomer who built his own observatory and wrote a book on the subject. Not a lot of people want to know that!

Billy Bennett

Charles Austin

Will Hay

George Robey and Max Miller were dream comedians for cartoonists. Sir George, the Prime Minister of Mirth, had wonderfully arched eyebrows and a cleric's hat and coat. He had made his stage debut back in 1891, but was still as sharp as a tack when I started sketching him in the early 1930s. I have never seen anybody to match him for timing. He used to speak thespian English, and walked the boundary lines of innuendo, pretending to be shocked at the audience's ability to find hidden meaning in the most innocent of remarks. Sir George, knighted in 1954, the last year of his life, could hold an audience in the palm of his hand, delivering his jokes in a confidential manner that gave everybody in the theatre the impression that he was talking one-to-one.

Sir George Robey

Max Miller was much brasher and worked at a quicker pace. He always told his audiences while pirouetting round the stage, 'Take a good look, lady. You'll never see another like me.' He was so right. I vividly recall the first time I sketched him at his local Brighton theatre. He made his stage entrance on a camel, and milked five minutes of hilarious business just trying to get off it. As he finally dismounted, he removed his fur-trimmed top coat to show off his floral plus fours and a silk jacket that was all the colours of the rainbow. The theatre was in uproar and he had not yet uttered a single joke. Like George Robey, much of his humour lay in what he didn't say as much as what he did say. He would leave the punch-lines to the imagination of his audience. As they roared at what were obviously suggestive thoughts he had cheekily planted he would put his hands on his hips, stare out at them, shake his head and say, 'My, my, what minds you've got.' He used to get in trouble for being blue, but by today's standards he was spotlessly clean. You'll never see another like him.

Max Miller

It was at Windsor that I first met Noël Coward, at the annual Royal Garden Party given by King George V and Queen Mary. The Master was

17

This montage for the 1934 Royal Command Performance was featured on the front page of The Era, *and got me noticed. I was about to sketch bandleader Jack Hylton, who was surrounded by song pluggers. He said, 'Have you finished yet?' 'I haven't even started,' I replied. 'But you could have drawn the entire ruddy band by now,' he said. We became good friends, and one of my outstanding memories is of him playing the piano for Maurice Chevalier in the old Press Club just off Fleet Street. It would have cost a fortune to get these two entertainment giants together, but they performed for free.*

A 'WAIST' OF TIME!

I have learned to flatter rather than fatten women, but even at nineteen I was showing no mercy to men in the never-ending battle of the bulge. This cartoon appeared in Wireless Weekly *in 1934.*

with Jessie Matthews, and as I sketched them he said, 'Do as you wish with me, young man, but make sure you are kind to darling Miss Matthews or I personally will see to it that your pencil is stuck in a quite unspeakable place.' Only he could make 'un-speak-able' sound like three threatening words.

This brings me to a confession. I have never felt completely comfortable drawing women. It goes back to an experience I had while scribbling for the *Southend Times*. The editor hired me out for the Mayor of Southend's garden party as a quick-sketch artist. It was all in aid of charity, and so I went along with it. I must have done more than one hundred rapid sketches during the afternoon, giving the drawings to the 'sitters' in exchange for a donation to the Mayor's fund. I had already established a style for myself in which I exaggerated any characteristic, so a big nose would become bigger, large ears would become elephantine and wide bottoms would become positively colossal. Oh dear, the ladies I do not make-a them laugh. The men loved my cartoon creations of them, but their wives struggled to see the funny side. It made me very wary of drawing women, and I tended in future to try to flatter rather than fatten them.

Fleet Street started to beckon after my 1934 montage of the Royal Command Performance had been projected on the front page of *The Era*. I submitted a series on London life to the *Star*, which was then a hugely successful evening newspaper that was locked in a bitter circulation war with the *Evening News* and *Evening Standard* in the days when London had three newspapers battling for the evening market. Suddenly a staff job came up for a cartoonist in the *Star* sports department, and I was on a shortlist of two for the post. My rival was a gifted artist called Barry Appleby, who was later to become my stablemate on the *Daily Express* with his incredibly popular everyday story of *The Gambols* that he created with his wife, Babs.

It was a toss up which one of us would get the job. The editor of *The Star* left the decision to the paper's highly regarded senior cartoonist Leslie Grimes, famous for his All My Own Work series.

Leslie considered Barry the better technician, but told the editor that my work had a touch of individuality about it that would give the *Star* sports pages a distinctive look. I got the job on a month's trial at the National Union of Journalists minimum wage of six guineas a week.

I was barely twenty, and there was a lot of lead in my pencil.

2: Reaching for the Star

MY EARLY FLEET STREET DAYS
AS A YOUNG MAN ABOUT TOWN,
GETTING DRUNK WITH ALEX
JAMES, MEETING GENERAL
FRANCO, AND DRIVING AT
BROOKLANDS WITH BANDLEADER
BILLY COTTON. WHAT A LIFE!

FLEET STREET in the 1930s. I felt like a character out of Evelyn Waugh's novel, *Scoop*. This was the exciting, intoxicating, never-sleeping Street of Ink, where nearly every building seemed to shake to the foundations with the thunder of printing presses rolling out the latest news. Fleet Street had a smell, a sound, a feel and a pace all of its own. Every time you stepped off the pavement you took your life in your hands as dozens of newspaper vans raced with each other to be first to get the newspapers to their vendors. This was life with the accelerator to the floor. Fleet Street was fifty miles from Westcliff as the crow flies, but it might as well have been a million miles. It was the most dynamic place I had ever visited in my life. I had been given a passport to paradise.

The *Star* editorial department was in the same office block as its sister paper, the *News Chronicle*. We were based at the Thames Embankment end of Bouverie Street, which is a tributary of Fleet Street. Come out of El Vinos, turn right and you will quickly find it. Mind you, a lot of my colleagues would come staggering out of El Vinos and not know where they were. These were heavy-drinking, fast-living, liver-destroying days. And there I was, twenty years old and full of myself. I stood a willowy six foot two in my polished brogues, but felt nine feet tall. My mind goes into a delightful spin just thinking back on it all.

After my month's trial, sports editor Arthur Williams said he was delighted with my work and took me on the staff at a princely nine guineas a week. That was something like double the national average wage. I managed to make such an impression that within six months my pay packet was increased to twelve guineas a week. I felt as if I owned Fleet Street.

In keeping with my new image, I rented a ten-guineas-a-month bachelor flat over a bank at Lancaster Gate which was equidistant to Fleet Street and the West End clubs and hotels where I danced away many a night to the music of such bands as Roy Fox, Jack Hylton, Geraldo and Edmundo Ros. A young man about town had to have suitable transport to get about town, and I bought myself the first of more than twenty cars that I have owned. It was a fourth-hand biscuit-coloured Singer with a gleaming chromium radiator, a wind-down roof and pump-up pneumatic seats. It cost me twenty pounds. I bought it from a garage in Highgate Hill, free-wheeled down the Hill while I got used to the controls and then drove it at snail-pace to Fleet Street. My only previous driving experience had been at the wheel of the car of a friend. Within two years I was tearing around the famous Brooklands racing track in the company of bandleader Billy Cotton, who raced a 200mph Riley with considerable skill and success. I also sat in Malcolm Campbell's record-breaking Bluebird racing car at Brooklands, but had more sense than to try it out on those banked Brooklands bends.

Like all those drivers from my generation, we did not have to pass a test. When the Ministry of Transport at last decided to protect the general public from the madmen at the wheel by introducing the driving test in 1935 I was the guinea-pig selected to take the test for a feature in the *Star*. I passed first time. By then I was driving a second-hand Riley sports car that had wooden floorboards. One night on the way back from a 1938 boxing show at Harringay (in which

LONSDALE BELTERS!
PHILLIPS AND HARVEY MEET TONIGHT FOR THE HEAVYWEIGHT CHAMPIONSHIP.

the defensive master Len Harvey regained the British heavyweight title from Eddie Phillips) I drove through a rain storm. It was then that I discovered the wooden floorboards were leaking and that we were taking on water at a Titanic rate. When I dropped off my passenger, a sweet young thing whose name escapes me, her silk stockings were soaked up to the calves. I never saw her again, and I think it fair to say that her interest in me shrunk.

A Midlands car dealer convinced me that I should never again buy a second-hand car, and talked me into paying out £200 for a maroon Austin 12 with leather upholstery. He waved me off from his Birmingham showroom, forty crisp white fivers swelling his pocket. Within a mile, the lights had failed, the carburettor had flooded and I had a puncture. When the war came I parked the car under railway arches near the home in Golders Green to which my parents had moved, and I eventually sold it to a doctor for fifty quid.

My early sports cartooning was confined to London, but this gave me a lot of scope because it was one of the sporting capitals of the world. I got particularly close to Alex James, one of the all-time great inside-forwards who made the outstanding Arsenal team of the 1930s tick with passes that were so precise that they were like arrows to the heart of a defence.

This was drawn after a war of a League match at Highbury in 1936. Arsenal manager George Allison commentated on the match for the BBC.

Our friendship flourished through a mutual love of golf, and we often played against each other at South Herts Golf Course, where young Dai Rees was the professional. Alex never used to bother with a tee peg, he would simply make a small divot in the grass with the heel of his club and then tee his ball up on it. I did not want to embarrass the great man by putting down a wooden tee, and so I copied his example. I was just about to drive off at the first on one particular afternoon when an elderly man in an ankle-length raincoat approached us from the direction of the clubhouse holding up a hand like a traffic policeman. 'Young man,' he boomed. 'I know who you are, and you should know better than to tee the ball up like that. Always use a peg. You will get a much better drive.'

I blushed as I blurted out a 'thank you'. He then returned to the clubhouse while I wondered if I was the first person to get a free lesson from none other than Harry Vardon, the master who invented the most commonly used golf grip.

Alex James, as famous for his knee-length baggy shorts as his ball skill, was not the best of influences on me. The wee Scot used to take me to an afternoon drinking club in Covent Garden where he would get legless and then rely on me to drive him home. This was commonplace on a Thursday, with a First Division match just forty-eight hours away. But on the Saturday he would play a blinder, and I quickly realised that alcohol to Alex was like petrol in his engine.

The name Alex James could open any door, and I had evidence of this when he took me to a leading Piccadilly gentlemen's outfitters and talked the manager into presenting me with a Jaeger overcoat worth twenty pounds. In return, I gave the manager an original, framed drawing of Alex. That overcoat warmed my back for more than ten years.

I was one of a dozen dedicated pipe smokers on the *Star*, and there was a permanent screen of smoke over the editorial department. Our Sports Editor Arthur Williams had a huge tobacco jar on his desk, and always contested that he could smoke a stronger mixture than any of us. I quietly encouraged the copy 'boys' – several of them older than me – to put him to the test. They cut up the rubber heel of a shoe and, while Arthur was on a break, pushed the pieces into the tobacco jar. For the following week Arthur puffed contentedly on his favourite old pipe without once commenting on the different taste. The place reeked of burning rubber.

The 1930s was the decade of the best of British in the shape of Fred Perry on the tennis court, Henry Cotton on the golf course, Joe Davis at the snooker table, Len Hutton at the batting crease, Jack Beresford in the rowing boat and Stanley Matthews on the wing for Stoke City and England. I do not wish for this book to come across as an exercise in name dropping, but it is a fact that all of these giants of the sports arena became good friends of mine. Writing colleagues used to have off-and-on relationships with the sporting heroes as their words struck home like poisoned darts, but I rarely managed to damage any friendships with cartoons that were sometimes critical but never ever cruel.

Fred Perry and I remained pals right up to his passing in 1995. The last time we were together he told me how an armed mugger had threatened him in a New York street. Fred, well into his seventies, pushed him to one side as if serving with his mighty right arm, and then legged it the three hundred yards to his hotel. 'I went and hid in my hotel room wondering whether the mugger had followed me,' he said. 'I was wearing a gold watch that had been presented to me after my third Wimbledon victory, and *nobody* was going to take that off me.'

Just before the war Fred gave me a short-sleeved shirt that he had designed. 'This,' he said, 'is going to make me my fortune.' I was most unimpressed, and I teased him by saying, 'Fancy a Labour MP's son having such capitalist ideas!' I thought that if he was going to plough his money into it he would lose his shirt. After the war, of course, Fred Perry sports shirts were in demand around the world. Wrong again, Ullyett.

I spent hours watching Joe Davis compile his breaks at the snooker table. He was just untouchable, and I would rate him higher than today's stars because he had perfected his skill with regular marathons at the billiards table where cueing control and accuracy is so vital. I once saw Joe make a billiards break of 1,013. His opponent Sydney Lee did not get off his seat for an entire session. It was an

Joe Davis

Fred Perry

incredible exhibition of cueing. Joe was continually being challenged in side stake matches, and I never once knew him come second best except occasionally against his younger brother, Fred, when he was not sufficiently motivated. Nobody could beat him at the snooker table off a level start.

Joe used to tell me that his cue was as special to him as any of my favourite pens were to me. He bought it in 1923 from a pal at the Palace Church Institute in Chesterfield. It cost him seven shillings and sixpence (37.5p), and he went on to win fifteen world snooker championships with it. I smile quietly to myself when I hear the likes of Stephen Hendry and Steve Davis being mentioned as the greatest snooker players of all time. Take it from me, Joe was Untouchable.

Jack Hobbs joined the *Star* just a few weeks after me, following his retirement from cricket. He was one of my boyhood heroes, and one of the few batsmen that could be mentioned in the same breath as Don Bradman. I used to accompany Jack and his ghost, Bill Evans, to Test matches, and I remember that in the mid-1930s he was the first to tell me to watch out for an unknown Middlesex batsman who had won a Jack Hobbs bat from the *Star* while batting for his Hendon school side. His name was Denis Compton.

When I went to cover live events, I was accompanied by an art room assistant in a van loaded with a photo-telegraphy machine, a Muirhead. It was an electromagnetic drum that, by using radio signals, could send photographs and cartoons through the airwaves back to the office. I would carry a narrow leather case with me in which I kept a collection of 2B pencils, a selection of brushes that I used like a pen, and also crayons, charcoal and a bottle of black artist's

RECORDING WITH HIS PEN
RECORDS WITH HIS BAT!

This was my welcome to Jack Hobbs when he joined the Star *team just a few weeks after me. On the right is a study of The Master at his desk.*

ink. On photo-telegraphy assignments I would use a fairly flimsy paper so that it would curl round the heated drum. There were several nightmare times when the paper would become bubbled and trapped in the drum, and I would hastily have to produce a substitute drawing from scratch. It can be a hard life, being a cartoonist (he lied).

This method of sending a cartoon for publication was fairly novel in the 1930s, and the *Star* used to put a 'by wire' line beneath my work. This, of course, meant nothing to the reader, but it told the opposition that we were on the ball with state-of-the-art technology. Nowadays, of course, everything is sent whooshing back to the office by modem to a computer screen. This is all double Dutch to me, and I also hear of cartoonists who use computers to help them compile their work. Give me the old pen-and-paper method any day. There is nothing to beat the challenge of facing a virgin sheet of paper or cardboard and having to fill it in a matter of deadline-meeting minutes. I am often asked how long it takes to draw a cartoon. I always reply, 'How long have I got?' I have always worked to deadlines, and have completed drawings in under ten minutes and have also taken an hour when I have had the luxury of not having a sports editor screaming for my work.

I was at the the Oval when Len Hutton scored his then world record 364 runs in the 1938 Test against Australia. It took more than thirteen hours, and when I asked Len how he felt at the end of it all he said in heavy Yorkshire: 'Bloody tired.' Not as tired, I bet, as Australian spin bowler Chuck Fleetwood-Smith, who conceded a record 298 runs for the reward of just one wicket. The cartoon that I sent back to the *Star* from the Oval to mark Hutton's marathon innings depicted cricket as a funny old game. For years old-timers had told us that modern England players were not in the same class as their predecessors. Now here they were finally being silenced by a pugnacious, twenty-two-year-old batsman from Pudsey, who was a man of few words but hundreds of runs. It suddenly seemed as if most of the spectators in the sell-out crowd had Yorkshire ancestry. As Hutton overtook Bradman's all-time Test record, the ground in Kennington, south London, erupted with choruses of the Yorkshire anthem, *On Ilkley Moor Baht 'At*. You could tell the Londoners who were joining in. They were singing 'On Hill Clear More By Tat'.

I was always amused by Hutton's no-holds-barred bluntness. He used to get straight to the point when under interrogation about an innings from media men desperate for a quote. There was one press conference when a journalist tried to persuade him to describe what had happened when he had been clean bowled by a ball from Keith Miller. 'Was it that the ball came in to you, or was it leaving you?' he was asked. Len appeared to give the question great consideration, and then said, 'I missed it.' He was sparing with his praise, but used to drop some beautiful one liners that were a joy for inspiration-seeking cartoonists like myself. He once said of Walter Hammond, 'Whenever I saw him batting I felt sorry for the ball.' He was a one off, was Our Len.

Prince Alexander Obolensky was another unique character. I saw the exiled Russian, who survived the Revolution by escaping with his family to England, score his two fantastic tries against New Zealand at Twickenham in 1936. I was

Len Hutton, silencing the ghosts of England's cricketing past with his 364 runs

then sent on a special assignment to watch him play for Richmond against Leicester, and the only pass he got all afternoon was when the trainer gave him

half a lemon to suck at half-time. He was a Prince by birth and a Prince in stature. I have rarely seen such an imperious looking sportsman. What a tragedy when Obo was killed when his RAF Hawker Hurricane crashed in the opening months of the Second World War.

One of my earliest cartoons for the *Star* featured Gordon Richards, the king of jockeys whom I depicted riding a bookmaker after he had caned the bookies by riding no less than twelve winners in succession. Gordon was a grand little man, and he had me chuckling in his days as a trainer with a true story about how Fleet Street reporters were hunting a story that he was seriously ill and had been whipped off in top secrecy to hospital.

'Reporters were chasing around trying to find out what was wrong with me and obituaries were being prepared,' he said. 'I then allowed the hospital to issue a short statement - "Gordon Richards, after many years of riding on very wet saddles, has been successfully treated for piles!"'

Prince Obolensky

Stanley Matthews nearly outlasted my pencil. He was a favourite subject of mine throughout his playing days from the early 1930s through to his final First Division game at the age of fifty back at Stoke where it had all started for him thirty-three years earlier.

Stanley took exception to one of my cartoons [see facing page] when I suggested that he was holding a gun to the Stoke City directors shortly before his transfer to Blackpool for £11,500 in 1947. But this was soon forgotten, and he used to make regular contact asking for originals of my cartoons featuring him.

Gordon Richards

28

This was the cartoon to which Stanley Matthews took exception. The popular view in the press was that Stanley was holding a gun to the heads of the Stoke City directors. He had been left out of the first team and demanded, 'Play me, or sell me.' Stoke sold him to Blackpool a month later for £11,500. In these more enlightened times it is clear that it was the clubs who were holding guns to the heads of players in an era when they were treated like slaves.

29

ROY ULLYETT: While There's Still Lead in My Pencil

The Wizard of Dribble was noted for making rather than taking goals, and it is a little-remembered fact that he once scored a hat-trick for England against Czechoslovakia at White Hart Lane in 1937. What was remarkable about it is that this very right footed player scored all three goals with his left as he pulled England back into a game that seemed lost for a dramatic 5-4 victory. You could always count on Stanley to provide something to write (and draw) about.

Jack Beresford was the Steven Redgrave of his day. He carried the British flag in the march past at the opening ceremony of the 1936 Berlin Olympics, the Games that Hitler and his cohorts managed to turn into a propaganda platform for the Nazi Party. Jack, who was competing in his fifth Olympiad and about to win his fifth Olympic medal, said later: 'If any of us in the British team had known what horrors Hitler had in store for the world, I am sure we would have got one of our rifle marksmen to have taken him out there and then. I shudder when I think how he gave the Nazi salute to the Union Jack as we walked past.' Jack, and his partner Leslie Southwood, had the Union Jack flying higher than the Swastika in the double sculls when they came from behind to beat the German favourites to take the gold medal.

Jack Beresford

In that same year I had a chance meeting with another notorious fascist leader. A Westcliff neighbour of mine, Rammy Brittan, whose father was the commodore at the local yacht club, was a cruise director for Canadian Pacific. He arranged for me to go on a cruise to the Canary Islands in the summer of 1936. On going ashore at Tenerife with a merry gang of English tourists on their first trip abroad, we found ourselves surrounded by Spanish soldiers angrily burning copies of British newspapers, including the *News Chronicle*, sister paper of *The Star*. I kept very quiet about my connections!

Their leader, a dumpy little man in jackboots and sporting an Oliver Hardy moustache, told us through an interpreter that we should take the message back home that Spaniards did not take kindly to British imperialists meddling in Spanish affairs. They objected to the way the British press were covering the civil unrest on the Spanish mainland. It turned out that the leader was none other than General Francisco Franco. A month later he left the Canary Islands to lead his troops at the start of the Spanish Civil War. The Spanish soldiers became quite friendly after the warm welcoming party, and as a memento of our meeting gave each of us a bullet to take home with us. I often wondered how many of them survived the bloody Civil War that Hitler and Mussolini used as a testing ground for a rather larger affair.

My lifetime love of boxers – not necessarily boxing – started in the 1930s when I mixed with the likes of Tommy Farr, Jack Petersen, Len Harvey, Eric Boon, Dave Crowley and Larry Gains. Boxers are a breed apart. People who never get to meet them tend to think they have their brains in their fists, but you will be surprised at how many intelligent men take up the hardest sport of all. Farr and Petersen, for instance, were Welshmen with an almost poetic way with words, and Harvey used to work out his tactics for a fight like a field marshal preparing a battle strategy.

I used to get to greet all the overseas boxers brought in as opponents, and my favourite was the former world heavyweight champion Max Baer. He could talk the ears off an elephant, and had a joke for every occasion. Max fell in love with London when he came over for 1937 fights against Tommy Farr and then South African Ben Foord. He told me that his ambition was to own a London hotel, and he asked me if I could find out if any were for sale. I spent a day contacting estate agents, and finally found a sixty-room hotel that was for sale just off Covent Garden. I went and viewed it as the official representative for 'an anonymous' American buyer, and satisfied myself that it

Max Baer

was the sort of first-class residence with which Max would want to be associated. Then I called Max at the Savoy, only to be told that he had checked out at short notice and had returned to the United States. Years later when I bumped into him at ringside in New York, I reminded him that he had wanted a hotel and that I had found him one. 'Jeez, Roy,' he said with a Broadway-wide grin, 'I didn't think you'd fall for that one. I say that every place I go.'

Max was a joker to the end. He died of a heart attack in 1959 the day after

31

refereeing a fight. He collapsed in his hotel room, and a passing bell boy said, 'Do you want a house doctor?' Max's last words were, 'I'd rather you got me a people doctor.'

The sportsman to whom I was always closest was golf genius Henry Cotton. He and his South American-born wife, Toots, were wonderful hosts, and always went out of their way to make my wife and I feel like part of their family. Henry did me the honour of inviting me to illustrate his instructional golf book. It became a massive best seller, and remains in my biased opinion one of the finest teaching books ever published on the most wonderful and most infuriating game ever invented. I used to spend hours with him in his plush home at Eaton Square where he was always dabbling in oils. He really fancied himself as an artist and one day asked me for an honest opinion of his work that adorned the walls of his lounge. As I was giving my view, Toots came into the room. 'Oh, Roy,' she said, in her charming accent, 'don't tell me that you are telling Henry what a wonderful painter he is. He gets everybody filling his ears with lies. They are all frightened to tell him the truth.'

'But, darling,' Henry protested, 'Roy has just pulled my work to pieces.'

'Well you did ask for an honest opinion,' I said.

Toots applauded. 'Well done, Roy,' she said. 'It's about time somebody put him in his place.'

Our friendship survived the criticism, but Henry got his own back. We were playing golf together at Wentworth and my game was in a terrible state. After illustrating the book and taking on board all the points Henry had made, I found that my mind was just too cluttered with technical detail. After I had shanked a shot off the tee, Henry looked at me with a twinkle in his eye and said, 'Let's face it, Roy. I can't paint. You can't play golf.'

I have rarely met anybody with as searching a mind as Henry had. He always went into great depth with any subject that took his interest. I was walking through Chelsea with him one afternoon when he stopped and watched a dustman lifting an overflowing dustbin and emptying it into the cart. He went over to the dustman and said, 'My man, I am lost in admiration for what you do. Would you mind if I examined your muscles?'

Just as the dustman was considering whether to hit Henry with his fist or the dustbin, I stepped in and explained just who he was and about his interest in muscle development. Henry was trying to work out why it was that so many golfers had back problems when swinging a club, yet people like this dustman could toss around loaded bins without any trouble. So there, in the middle of a Chelsea side street, Henry Cotton – Britain's greatest golfer of any time, in my view – examined the back and shoulder muscles of a dustman.

We remained close buddies up to his death at Christmas 1987. Wherever he

TO HAVE AND TO HOLED!

HENRY COTTON IS OUT TO RETAIN HIS 'OPEN'
TITLE AT SANDWICH

My dear old friend Henry Cotton won the British Open three times: in 1934, 1937 and 1948. His victory in 1937 was particularly outstanding because every member of the United States Ryder Cup team took part. Henry will always be remembered for his round of 65 on his way to winning the Open at Sandwich in 1934. It inspired the popular golf ball, the 'Dunlop 65'. Henry really fancied himself as a painter. The one certain fact is that he was an artist when he held a golf club in his hands.

This was the jacket that I drew (right) for the exceptionally successful instructional book by Henry Cotton. It was one of the first of its kind, and typical of Henry that he should be in at the pioneering stage. The book was unique in that Henry's personal tips appeared in his own hand writing along with the conventional text. At Henry's insistence, I included some humorous drawings to underline how NOT to play the game. Henry may not have shown it when he was playing, but he had a lovely sense of humour.

Henry Cotton says...

'PLAY BETTER GOLF —
These tips have helped me
and hundreds of my pupils'

ILLUSTRATED by Roy Ullyett.

was in the world he would send me a postcard with a cryptic message. One of the last said, 'I hope you've still got lead in your pencil.' Just about, Henry old friend. Just about.

I was lucky to be teamed with several writers at the *Star* who made my life easier by providing beautifully composed articles to accompany my cartoons. They included Bill Evans, Jack Ingham and F.W. Thomas, all of whom painted word pictures that gave a lift to my work.

The projection I was getting brought me to the attention of that new fangled invention *television*. I was invited to the BBC television studio at Alexandra

Palace in the winter of 1938 to talk about my work in a live broadcast. Of course, everything was live in those days because there was no such thing as tape.

The *Star* made a bit of a song and dance about the TV interest in me, and my colleague Leslie Grimes captured me with the drawing on the left. The overcoat is the one that I got free, thanks to Alex James! The Grimes portrait was accompanied by these words:

Roy Ullyett, whose sport cartoons have won a national public in the four years that he has been on the staff of the Star, *is to be televised while at work by the BBC at Alexandra Palace tomorrow. Roy goes everywhere in sport and knows everyone. His cartoons are eagerly sought by those whom he draws. They hang in sport headquarters, and in the homes of sport celebrities and all over the country. As recently as this morning Stanley Rous, the famous football referee and Football Association official, asked for the Ullyett cartoon in which he was featured. Roy Ullyett cartoons hang on walls of famous homes as far away as Australia, the United States and South Africa. They have become collectors' items. Cricketer Donald Bradman, boxer Max Baer and golfer Bobby Locke are just three of the many sports stars who have contacted the* Star *for the original Ullyett works of art featuring them. Fun without foolishness. Captions with a bite and a grin. Drawings that reveal a depth of sports knowledge and an insight into very human sports failings with, as often as not, a quite clear lesson in sport tactics. All with a laugh. That's Roy Ullyett.*

I am blushing as I read the words sixty years on. Somebody Up There at the *Star* Liked Me.

My television appearance, for an afternoon audience of all of three thousand viewers, was an ordeal. There was just one camera, and interviewer Leslie Mitchell stood off to my left while I had to give my answers to his questions into the camera to the right. I was stiffly positioned at a large drawing board and gave examples of lightning sketches of the likes of Tommy Farr, Max Baer and Joe Davis. A harassed floor manager was crawling on all fours underneath the camera and kept tugging at my trousers to make me turn to the camera and not block the view as I was drawing. It got to the stage where I was drawing without looking at the board! This would have made a great television comedy sketch. It was scorching under the television lights, and I was half expecting my art paper to go up in flames. I was paid five guineas for the interview, and felt as if I had lost ten pounds in weight. This television lark, I thought, will never catch on.

It amazed me that they managed to get any programmes out, just as I was often astonished that we managed always to get our newspapers on to the streets on time. The best laid plans often used to go wrong. One instance I particularly remember is when we decided to rush out a final edition with a back page lead report on the running of the first horse ever to carry the colours of George VI. This was just four days after the abdication of his brother Edward VIII. We knew we would not have time to get a photograph of the race in the paper, and so I was instructed to draw a suitable picture to illustrate what our racing department was convinced would be a Royal victory. The object of the exercise was to suck up to the new King! But all we managed to do was embarrass him, because his horse – Marconi

King George VI, a smiling loser

– finished eighth of nine runners, and it warranted no more than a paragraph.

My picture showed him grinning broadly as he looked on through binoculars. He certainly would not have been grinning, and he was nowhere near the Windsor course. We were stuck with the story as our lead, and the headline screamed: KING'S HORSE DISAPPOINTS WINDSOR CROWD. But not half as much as it disappointed our editor! Incidentally, Marconi ran for three kings. As a two-year-old he ran for George V, and was owned by Edward VIII before being transferred to George VI. Not a lot of people want to know that, either!

My talent, if that was what it was, had been spotted by other editors, and I started to get tugs to move to daily newspapers. But I was very content on the *Star*, particularly when they gave me permission to augment my salary by drawing on a regular basis for the *Sunday Pictorial*. I created two cartoon characters for the *Pic:* Humphrey, an overweight and over-enthusiastic sportsman who tried his hand at everything with disastrous results, and Bob Standing, a know-all fan who knew damn all.

The third of the three examples below of Humphrey at play was repeated in the *Pic* just two weeks later, after Charlton goalkeeper Sam Bartram had been left standing on his goal-line for fifteen minutes. The 1937 League match against Chelsea at Stamford Bridge had been abandoned because of fog. Nobody told poor old Sam, and they had to send a search party out for him.

I also had a weekly topical sports cartoon in the *Pictorial*, and my income

BOB STANDING - - -
Blowing Own Trumpet!

Bob Standing had a platform in the Sunday Pictorial ... *until Hitler interrupted.*

was allowing me to lead a very comfortable existence. It was, of course, too perfect to last.

The Ullyett good life was rudely interrupted on 3 September 1939 when Prime Minister Neville Chamberlain announced, 'We are at war with Germany.'

Even I found it difficult to find anything funny in that.

3: War on Two Fronts

EXEMPTION FROM WAR, AND THEN I SERVE IN THE ARMY AND THE RAF. I AM PASSED OFF AS AN ARCHBISHOP'S SON, FLY SKY HIGH IN OKLAHOMA AND MEET AND MARRY THE LOVE OF MY LIFE. LUCKY OLD CHAP.

AS a cartoonist, I was at first given early exemption from a call-up. It was considered that I could best help the war effort by keeping readers cheerful and firing some shots in the propaganda battle. My pen, it was decided, was considerably mightier than my sword. As you will see from the cartoons on the following pages, I managed to take some ego-puncturing swipes at Corporal Hitler and his henchmen. A couple of the originals found their way on to the walls of the War Ministry at Whitehall, so I must have been hitting the target.

I had been taking pot-shots at Hitler long before war was declared, and my personal favourite was a send-up of the Munich rallies when I had him pleading

for a ticket for the 1939 FA Cup Final at Wembley between Wolves and Portsmouth. This was the famous 'Monkey Gland Final' when, during the build-up, the Wolves players were given injections of a mystery substance allegedly taken from monkey glands. They were accused of doping their players, but it was Wolves who were left looking like dopes when the underdogs of Portsmouth pulverised them 4-1.

Everybody's lives turned upside down with the outbreak of war, yet with all the worry and anxiety I found people more eager to laugh and poke fun at life than during peacetime. Petrol and food

FUEL SHORTAGE IN GERMANY.

"FOR ADOLF'S SAKE STOP RATTLING THOSE MEDALS, HERMAN".
"THAT'S NOT MEDALS, IT'S MY TEETH CHATTERING!"

ROLL OUT THE BARREL

NO CARD FOR HITLER, SEND HIM A PIECE OF MISTLETOE

HE CAN STAND UNDERNEATH IT AND WONDER WHO THE HECK WOULD WANT TO KISS HIM.

"HERMAN, WE SHOULD HAVE RUN THIS WAR LIKE THE CAMBRIDGESHIRE. I'M TOLD THERE'LL BE TWO WINNERS."

HITLER IS PREPARED TO SACRIFICE A MILLION LIVES says a report.

"Isn't he splendid. With so much to occupy his mind he can spare a thought for each one of us."

HITLER CALLS HIS GENERALS — "WONDER WHAT HE CALLED THEM?"

"UNCLE GOEBBELS, IF MISTER CHURCHILL IS SUCH A RAT AS YOU SAY, WHY ISN'T HE A NAZI?"

"HUSH CHILD, EVEN I WOULDN'T WISH HIM THAT!"

rationing was introduced, there were daily blackouts, and a shortage of newsprint meant newspapers were limited for space. All the ingredients were there for total misery, but I know my memory is not playing tricks when I say that you could warm your hands on the spirit of the people.

The Football League programme was abandoned, and the sports scene became so bleak that I decided I needed a fresh approach to my cartooning. I put up an idea for a strip on a character called just plain Smith, a daily look at how an ordinary middle-aged Brit was coping with the crisis. He ran every day in the *Star* up to the start of the Blitz, and then it was all hands to the pump. Even a cartoonist was suddenly considered soldier material. I signed off in the *Star* with a strip in which I substituted for Smith, and featured my chum Leslie Grimes, with whom I shared an office, ideas and a laugh at life. I depicted myself with my feet up on my desk, which is the way it was in an office in which we were casual to the point of lethargy. The war was about to shake me out of this mode.

I secretly wanted to fly with the RAF, but went along with the suggestion that I would be best off in the Army. 'Your lanky legs would be too long for a Spitfire,' I was told. 'And, anyway, at twenty-seven you're too old to start flying.' I joined the Queen's Royal Regiment, after a medical examination during which the doctor exclaimed: 'Goodness, you've let yourself go to seed early. This is the body of an aging man.' It was a commentary on the Fleet Street good life.

After initial training at Surrey, I passed the officer's exam and was made up to a lieutenant. Looking back, I can safely say that my year in the Army was the most miserable time of my life. So far. It was all too robotic and unpalatable for my artistic tastes. I was one of the Many who admired the actions of the Few during the Battle of Britain, and when their Finest Hour was all over, the RAF

started a recruitment drive for pilots to replace those tragically lost in the triumph over the Luftwaffe.

My Commanding Officer was surprisingly understanding when I inquired about the possibility of a transfer to the RAF. I don't think he could wait to get shot of me. He told me: 'I am aware that you are like a duck out of water in the Army. There is, at times, an apparent relaxed manner in the RAF that we could not allow in the Army, but it will be more appropriate to your free spirit.'

He pointed to my moustache that was beginning to take on handlebar proportions, much like that favoured by many RAF types. 'I think you have already made a statement

A self-destruct portrait, 1943

41

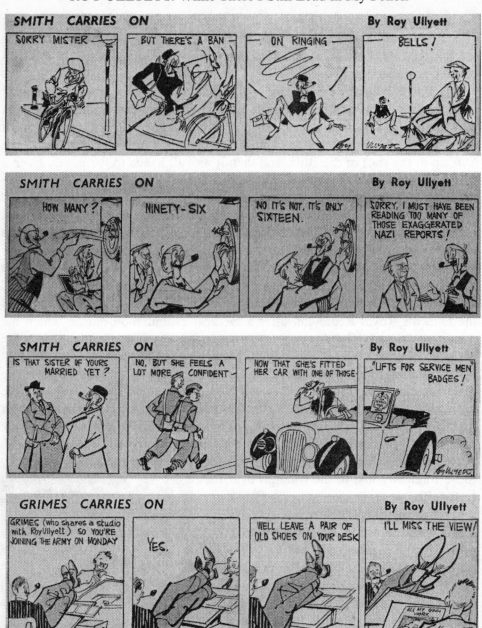

Smith carried on in the Star *for three months, until it was decided I would be better employed fighting the war rather than laughing at it. For my farewell to the* Star *I ditched poor old Smith and substituted Leslie Grimes, the cartooning master with whom I shared an office and who was a Fleet Street favourite because of his hilarious All My Own Work series.*

about your future,' he said. 'That's an RAF tash if ever I saw one.'

Lieutenant R.H.F. Ullyett, the Queen's Royal Regiment, resigned his commission, and within weeks was suddenly L.A.C. R.H.F. Ullyett, of the RAF Volunteer Reserve. After two months of basic training, I left with other volunteers on board the Queen Elizabeth – transformed into a troop ship – bound for Canada. We docked at Newfoundland, moved on to Ottawa, and then caught a Canadian National Railways train down to the United States. Destination: Miami ... but no, not Miami, Florida. We arrived in Miami, O-o-o-o-o-klahoma, where the corn is as high as an elephant's eye, in March 1943 for six months intensive pilot training at the Spartan School of Aeronautics. To us, it was No 3 British Flying Training School and I became the Under Officer on No 15 Course. I very nearly called it a crash course, which it sometimes threatened to be.

American air ace Chuck Wood, an Advanced Flying Instructor, was my tutor, and on our first couple of flights in a single-prop P.T.19 USAF fighter plane, he laid his tongue to every known anglo-Saxon swear word as I struggled to get the hang of things. It was quietly pointed out to him by colleagues that I was the son of an Archbishop, and his swearing was damaging sensitive ears. From then on, Chuck was a proper gentleman with me and coaxed me through the course without a word out of place. After my final lesson, he told me: 'God knows why, but I'm going to pass you and let you kill your silly self. It will be interesting to see whether you kill any Krauts before you kill yourself.' As he shook my hand, I let go with a torrent of swearing that turned the air blue. He then realised that perhaps I was not an Archbishop's son after all. Chuck took it in good part, and we had a swearing duel at ten paces which I am ashamed to report that I won. Fleet Street had got me well prepared for it.

At the end of the course, which included exhausting commando combat training, I was the fittest I had been in my life, and in a physical shape that would have amazed the Army doctor who diagnosed my early deterioration. After the strict rationing of England, the food in the ranching state of Oklahoma was unbelievable. Succulent steaks big enough to saddle a horse, and all the fresh vegetables you could eat. The Americans were incredibly hospitable, but we never lost sight of our first priority of getting our wings.

I managed to find time to cast an eye on the American sports scene, and guested as a cartoonist for the *Chicago*

BASEBALL IN ENGLAND ?
NOT WHILE PANTS ARE RATIONED !

43

"Listen in to the Stadium Club boxing?"
"No, too bloomin' rough for my liking!"

"TAKE THAT WHISTLE OFF THE KETTLE HONEY, THE NEIGHBOURS THINK IT'S AN AIR RAID!"

"DON'T YOU THINK WE MIGHT STOP DRESSING FOR DINNER NOW WE CAN'T KEEP THE CURTAINS OPEN?"

"HE'S RECOGNISED ME, I USED TO BE A FOOTBALL REFEREE."

I was ordered to try to make people laugh at the war. I did my best.

LAND ARMY TRACTOR GIRL UNABLE TO FORGET THAT SHE USED TO BE A HAIR DRESSER

Herald at a baseball match at Wrigley Park between the Chicago Cubs and the New York Yankees. It was my first insight into how commercialised sport could become, and how it was possible to give spectators first-class facilities instead of treating them like cattle, which was often the case back home. There was match and club sponsorship, executive boxes, convenient car parking facilities, all spectators were seated and there was a PR machine in place that made media work so much easier than in Britain, where doors tended to be shut in the face rather than opened to help with background information. It has taken something like fifty years for British sport to catch up and realise that it has to project and sell itself. But, just to show what a contradictory old so-and-so I am, I have to say I prefer the bumbling way it was. The well-meaning but bungling amateurs who ran our sports provided non-stop fodder for cartoonists, and I thank them from the bottom of my wallet.

My six months in the United States rushed by, mainly because we were giving so much concentration and effort to our intense training programme. We forged close links with the local people of Miami, who treated us like favourite sons, particularly as so many of their boys were away fighting the war in the Pacific. We were 'adopted' by a wealthy Kansas City lady called Mrs Paul. W. Jenkins, who was 'Mama Jenks' to all us boys on the Fifteenth Course. She used to drive us around in her huge black Packard saloon car with white-walled tyres, and saw to it that we visited rodeos, Indian reservations and the prairies to get a proper taste of American life. I have never known such an extraordinarily generous woman, and there is a permanent reminder of our bond with her in the Kansas City Community Church at Main and 46th Street, where we donated a chair from 'Mama Jenks's RAF Boys'.

I cannot hear a song from the wonderful Rodgers and Hammerstein musical

I guested as a sports cartoonist for the Chicago Herald. *They paid me peanuts!*

45

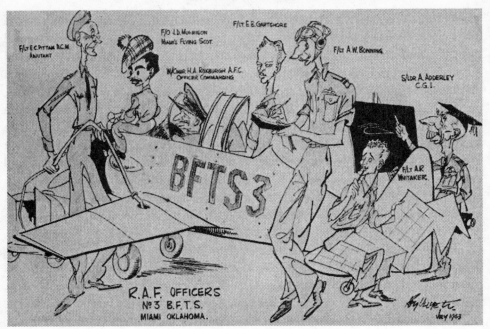

Memories of O-o-o-o-oklahoma. Top, the RAF officers who guided us to our wings. This drawing was framed and hung in the officers' mess. Bottom, my link instructor buddies on the course. They are depicted trying to keep cool in front of the temperamental air conditioning system during a summer when we fried.

Oklahoma! without feeling nostalgic for that period of my life. My abiding memory of Miami is of experiencing just about every extreme of weather. It was perishing cold when we arrived, then there was the worst flooding in the State's history when bridges were washed away, and this was followed by weeks on end of temperatures at one hundred and ten degrees fahrenheit. We all looked like Red Indians before the course finished, and would not have looked out of place on the nearby Quapaw Reservation.

I was Pilot Officer Ullyett by the time we sailed back to Blighty aboard the Queen Mary, and the war in Europe had taken a dramatic turn. The Germans were on the run and Churchill and his generals were plotting the D-Day invasion of Europe for June 1944. It was bomber pilots rather than fighter pilots who were in demand, and I was sent up to Scotland for what was a pretty uneventful posting. No wartime

heroics to report, I'm afraid. I just flew routine patrols, and, to my amazement, proved Chuck Wood wrong by coming back in one piece at the end of each flight.

At regular intervals, I used to travel down to London by train to visit my parents in Golders Green. I would arrive at King's Cross, take my bike from the guard's van and then cycle to north west London. Whenever there was a pretty girl's attention to be caught, I would ride no-hands style and hold on to my by now fully fledged handlebar moustache and pretend to steer the bike with it. Pilot Officer Ullyett coming into land. What a proper Charlie I must have looked!

In the spring of 1944 I was transferred to Harrogate for what proved the beginning of a love affair that has lasted for more than half a century. I was introduced to a fashion buyer from Bradford called Margaret Wright, and from the first moment I looked into her beautiful blue eyes I felt – how does that song from *Oklahoma*! go? – 'like I was climbing clear up to the sky'.

Maggie ran a small fashion shop in Bradford, and was recognised as one of the most discerning buyers in the business. Proof of it is that she was appointed by the British Board of Trade and Industry to boost export business that had come to a dead halt during the war. She and a handful of other fashion buyers used to visit the London fashion houses where, under the all-knowing eye of Norman Hartnell, they would choose the fashions and fabrics that they considered would find a market in the United States. It was all to help bring cash into the treasury coffers. Silks and chiffon that would never have seen the light of day in British shop windows during those stark days of clothing coupons were shipped off to America in return for desperately needed dollars.

One of the perks of Maggie's job was that she used to be put up in luxury at the Savoy during her buying weekends in London, and we waltzed away many a happy hour to the music of the Savoy Orpheans. We were on the dancefloor one evening when I said to Maggie, ''Don't look now. I'll turn us round so that you can see a sailor dancing.' Maggie expected it to be a sailor in a square collar, and was astonished to find herself dancing alongside Lord Louis Mountbatten in full naval uniform, partnering his wife.

Even at this distance, I become quite soppy when I recall how Maggie and I went to the see the 1945 opening night of Ivor Novello's new musical *Perchance to Dream* in the Strand. The show stopping song was *We'll Gather Lilacs in the Spring Again*. That was the night we declared undying love for each other, and that song remains the one that carries special meaning for us. Yes, I'm an old romantic. And why not? Mind you, on the whole I would rather be a young one.

Maggie and I decided we wanted to spend the rest of our lives together (which we have, so far). We had what was a customary wartime Register office wedding, and moved in with my parents at Golders Green while we decided where we would live once the war was over. I returned to my cartooning duties at the *Star* following VE Day, and when the lovely Freya came along in 1946 we elected to bring her up on the Essex coast at Westcliff rather than in The Smoke of London. Freya, or Tosh as we always called her, has been a perpetual light in our lives. She has managed to combine a successful career in the showbusiness management world (she created the New Seekers and among her clients are Shakin' Stevens and Mr Motivator) with bringing up two bright kids, Kate and Ben. Freya and her husband, John, have homes in Los Angeles, Majorca and, best of all, in the middle of the Yorkshire Dales, and are, along with the grandchildren, a great source of joy to both Maggie and me. Freya was the main driving force behind this book. So blame her, not me.

Slowly but surely the sports wheels got back in motion after we had been rudely interrupted by Hitler, and it was cartooning business as usual as Denis Compton and Bill Edrich filled the immediate post-war years with hundreds of runs, and bombed and blitzed London proudly pulled itself together to stage the 1948 Olympics. I was now on sixteen guineas a week with the *Star*, and supplemented my income by drawing a weekly cartoon for the *Sunday Pictorial* under the name of Berryman, which was a play on a nickname that I had for Maggie.

On the following pages I present a cross-section of my work that gives a feel of what was what and who was who on the British sports scene in the 1940s ...

My Sunday Newsreel by Berryman strip ran in the Sunday Pictorial *as a light look at the week's news in the immediate post-war years. The pram joke in the second strip refers to the arrival of Prince Charles in 1948. New mums throughout the country bought prams styled on the one in which Charles was being pushed around by his nanny.*

The first full year of sport after the war was one for the underdogs. The grey Airborne won the 1946 Derby at 50-1, backed by hundreds of ex-RAF servicemen, going totally on sentiment. According to the form book, Airborne did not stand a chance, but jockey Tommy Lowrey booted him home in a thrilling finish. An outsider was also a winner at Wimbledon. Yvon Petra, a 6 foot 7 inch Frenchman who learned his game playing barefoot in the steamy heat of French Indo-China, beat Australian Geoff Brown in the men's singles final. Brown served right-handed and returned the ball either left-handed or with both hands on the racket. Petra was a cartoonist's dream, with his Fernandel face and daddy-long-legs physique. He was a remarkable chap who after his unexpected victory gave the credit for his success to a German prison camp surgeon. Seriously wounded during the war, he was taken prisoner by the Nazis. Petra was in danger of having one of his long legs amputated, but it was saved on the operating table by the skills of the surgeon.

CUE-TIPPED
BY BROTHER
JOE TO WIN
HIS VACATED
SNOOKER
TITLE

Fred Davis

FRED DAVIS *finally managed to escape from the shadow of his legendary brother, Joe, in the immediate post-war years. When Joe stepped down after dominating the snooker scene from the mid-1920s, it was Fred who stepped into his shoes with eight world title successes. Twelve years younger than Joe, Fred never made the mistake of taking his sport too seriously and was always able to communicate a sense of fun and enjoyment to the spectators. He and Walter Donaldson contested eight consecutive world finals. Wee Walter became disillusioned with the game to the point where he turned the billiard room at his Buckinghamshire home into a cowshed and broke up the slates of his table to pave a path!*

No man looked less like a world beater than Sydney Wooderson, the tiny, bespectacled Camberwell solicitor who was Britain's best middle distance runner either side of the war. He was as white as a bottle of milk, and suffered poor health. Yet this was the man who won his way into the hearts of the nation with his courageous performances. His greatest victory came in 1946 after he had lost his best running years to the war. He won the European 5000 metres title in Oslo, beating a class field including Emil Zatopek. I named Woody Sportsman of the Year when there was no such title.

HE STANDS OUT MILES!
Sportsman OF THE YEAR

SYDNEY WOODERSON

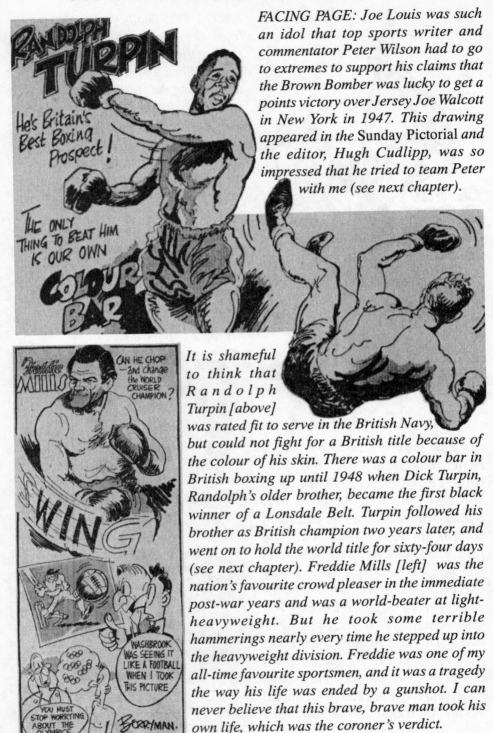

FACING PAGE: Joe Louis was such an idol that top sports writer and commentator Peter Wilson had to go to extremes to support his claims that the Brown Bomber was lucky to get a points victory over Jersey Joe Walcott in New York in 1947. This drawing appeared in the Sunday Pictorial and the editor, Hugh Cudlipp, was so impressed that he tried to team Peter with me (see next chapter).

It is shameful to think that Randolph Turpin [above] was rated fit to serve in the British Navy, but could not fight for a British title because of the colour of his skin. There was a colour bar in British boxing up until 1948 when Dick Turpin, Randolph's older brother, became the first black winner of a Lonsdale Belt. Turpin followed his brother as British champion two years later, and went on to hold the world title for sixty-four days (see next chapter). Freddie Mills [left] was the nation's favourite crowd pleaser in the immediate post-war years and was a world-beater at light-heavyweight. But he took some terrible hammerings nearly every time he stepped up into the heavyweight division. Freddie was one of my all-time favourite sportsmen, and it was a tragedy the way his life was ended by a gunshot. I can never believe that this brave, brave man took his own life, which was the coroner's verdict.

I enjoyed drawing horses, but I could not tip rubbish. Tudor Minstrel was, I thought, a racing certainty for the 1947 Epsom Derby, particulary with Gordon Richards on his back. But he finished a distant fourth behind three French horses led by Pearl Diver.

JEANETTE ALTWEGG was one of the most remarkable of all British sportswomen. She was better known in the immediate post-war year as a lawn tennis player and was runner up in the junior national championships. But she elected to put all her energy into ice skating, and finished fifth in the 1947 world championships, fourth in 1948, third in 1949, second in 1950 and, at last, first in 1951. She then won two European titles to go with the Olympic bronze medal she collected in 1948. Her peak performance came in the 1952 winter Olympics when she won the gold medal with a dazzling display of skating. She was offered professional deals, but preferred to hang up her skates to become a teacher at a children's orphanage in Switzerland. Jeanette was a very special lady.

IT rained runs in the summer of 1947 when Denis Compton set records galore that remain to this day. I cannot believe that anybody will ever beat his mighty collection of eighteen centuries, and his season's run haul of 3816 runs at an average 90.85. Compo, who became a revered colleague of mine on Express *Newspapers*, was also an FA Cup winning medallist with Arsenal. He shared much of his run harvest for England and Middlesex with Bill Edrich, who had been a DFC-winning war hero as a squadron leader, leading daylight bomber raids on Berlin. Both he and Denis were heroes on the cricket field.

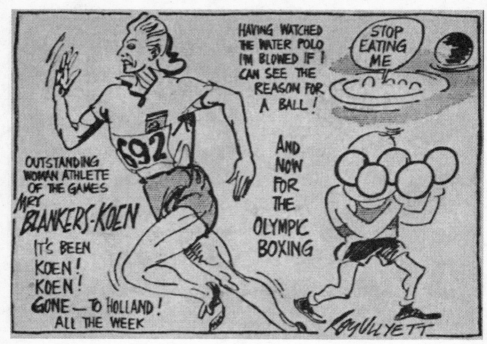

Flying Dutchwoman Fanny Blankers-Koen was the undisputed star of the 1948 London Olympics at Wembley Stadium with a haul of four gold medals. Fanny, a thirty-year-old housewife and mother of two, was coached by her husband, who motivated her with the deliberate taunt: 'They are saying you are too old, Fanny. Go out and prove them wrong.' There was plenty of material for cartoon comedy during the Games. In the gymnastics competition, for instance, the judging was, to say the least, fairly eccentric. The maximum that can be scored for any one exercise is 10.00. One judge was removed from the panel when she awarded a score of 13.1!

Frank Swift was the first goalkeeper to captain England. He was a magnificent last line of defence when England beat Italy 4-0 in Turin in 1948. Frank, a lovely larger-than-life character, tragically died in the 1958 Munich air crash when, travelling as a newspaperman, he thumbed a lift on the plane at the last minute.

Don Bradman's 1948 Australians were arguably the greatest team ever to visit these shores. They went through their tour without a single defeat, and they saved their most savage display for a visit to my home town of Southend-on-Sea. In a single day at Southchurch Park they scored a record 721 runs. That was the match in which Keith Miller went to the wicket with nearly 400 runs already on the board. Facing his first ball from my good pal and neighbour Trevor Bailey, he raised his bat and allowed the ball to hit his stumps. He was too much of a caring sportsman to want any part of the massacre. Bradman was such an incredible run machine that it used to make front page headlines on the rare occasions when he failed to score. His most famous duck was in his final Test against England at The Oval in 1948. He was bowled second ball by Eric Hollies when needing just four run for a perfect average of 100.

Here I am (left) at nine, with the drawing-board of life ahead of me. That's my brother Norman with me. Sadly, he died in India of a fever when he was twenty-three.

My mother, pretty as a picture.

Lazy, hazy days on the Norfolk Broads.

The picture above was taken in my young man-about-town days, when I came under the wing of the fabulous Arsenal forward Alex James (right).

'Pon my soul! This was taken on my last day at the Star *before going to war in 1940. My shoes were for sale at four shillings and sixpence. The next day it was Army boots.*

War on two fronts. That's me as Lieutenant R.H.F. Ullyett of the Queen's Regiment (right) and, eighteen months later, as Flight Officer R.H.F. Ullyet of the RAF Volunteer Force.

The love of my life. This is Maggie and I about to gather lilacs during a wonderful lifetime together. Maggie has given me the best fifty-plus years of my life, so far.

Boxing was always my favourite spectator sport. Here I am with some all-time greats: Jack Dempsey and Des Hackett (top), Harry 'The Nose' Levene and Rocky Marciano (above) and Sugar Ray Robinson (right).

An unlikely trio march down the fairway at Sunningdale in the Bowmaker Pro-am at Sunningdale in 1959. That's South African golf master Bobby Locke (centre), and on the left Christopher Lee, a scratch player who was no sucker on the golf course. I was within inches of a hole in one. As the crowd applauded, I overheard a spectator say: 'About time he hit a decent bloody shot!'

Who's this handsome chap? Goodness, I do believe it's me in 1989 on the day I heard I had been awarded an OBE.

I am about to drive the ball the little matter of 410 metres ... in a competition to mark the opening of a new runway at Palma Airport.

A chuckle of cartoonists, helping me celebrate twenty-one years in Fleet Street. The pen masters are, from left to right: Barry Appleby (famous for his Gambols strip in the Express), *the witty and waspish Sir Osbert Lancaster, the legendary Carl Giles (note that face, on which he based his Grandma Giles!), and, on my left, JAK, who was a genius of a laughtermaker on the* Evening Standard.

What a laugh. I collect my Cartoonist of the Year award from the Duke of Bedford in 1961. The award was organised by the exclusive Cartoonists' Club.

King Rat Davy Kaye (right) looks on as I meet Prince Philip at a Grand Order of Water Rats charity fund-raising dinner.

My favourite photograph of Prince Charles, taken on the day in 1975 that he joined me as a Companion of the Water Rats.

Happy family. This is me with my favourite people. That's the marvellous Maggie on my right, and our daughter Freya on the far left. In between are my granddaughter Kate, grandson Ben and son-in-law John. Quite a few years earlier, Freya (right) was already piping up with the sort of personality that has made her a powerful force in the entertainment management business.

THE FINAL STRAW AT LORD'S

I'm afraid it was all too easy to raise laughs at England's expense during the 1948 tour by Sir Donald Bradman's unbeatable Australians.

Billy Wright, the driving captain of Wolves and England, led Wolves to the FA Cup in 1949. He was a magnificent field marshal, captaining Wolves to a procession of memorable triumphs and leading England 90 times while winning a then record 105 caps. Billy was often on the receiving end of my pencil, and always went out of his way to thank me for taking the trouble to draw him. A real solid-gold gentleman.

Bobby Locke was a dear friend of mine, and we spent many happy hours together on and off the course. He won the British Open title four times with a style that was all his own. His speciality was a wide sweeping hook that always made the ball look as if it was going yards off target but would then suddenly swing in and land bang on target. If I had to choose a man to putt for my life, it would be Bobby, who was THE master on the green.

Johnny Leach was world table tennis champion in 1949 and 1951. He perfected his game, like many of us, while serving in the RAF. Most of us hung up our bats once the war was over, but Johnny went on to conquer the world at ping pong. He was the last Englishman to win the world title.

Reg Harris was, without question, Britain's greatest ever track sprint cyclist. He had thighs like tree trunks that were a magnet for sports cartoonists. His training for the 1948 Olympics was handicapped by a broken arm, and he had to be satisfied with two silver medals. He then turned professional and won the world title at his first attempt. Seventeen years after his retirement in 1957 he made an amazing return to racing in 1974, and won the British sprint championship at 54.

I did a lot of freelance work for boxing promoters, particularly for the great showman Jack Solomons, who was Britain's Mr Boxing in the immediate post-war period. He was continually searching for a British-born world heavyweight champion, but his best hope – Bruce Woodcock – did not quite have the ammunition when he mixed in the best company against the top Americans. This, of course, was in the good old days when there was only one champion in each weight division. I know that I am not alone in being totally confused by today's alphabet championship pantomime.

4: Expressing Myself

THE EXPRESS PINCH ME FROM
UNDER THE NOSE OF THE MIRROR,
I DOUBLE MY MONEY, REPORT THE
TORPEDOING OF TURPIN IN NEW
YORK, TEAM UP WITH THE MAN IN
THE BROWN BOWLER, AND LIVE
LIKE A MILLIONAIRE.

FLEET STREET legend Hugh Cudlipp was always telling me that I should have a national stage for my work. It was the dynamic Cudlipp who, in his role as editor, encouraged me to freelance with the *Sunday Pictorial* under the pen name of Berryman. Early in the 1950s he decided that he wanted me full-time on his staff, and he confided that the *Pic* was to have a title change to the *Sunday Mirror* and would have closer ties with its sister paper, the best-selling *Daily Mirror*. His idea was that I should become the sports cartoonist for *both* papers. 'Let's talk about it over lunch,' he said.

As we walked together towards the Albany Club, where Cudlipp had booked a table, he chatted excitedly in his lovely Welsh lilt about his plans that included me as a roving cartoonist with the world of sport as my oyster. 'I will team you with Peter Wilson,' he said. 'The Man They Can't Gag with the Cartoonist with A Gag for Every Occasion.' His impressive flow was interrupted by the sight of a *Mirror* PR girl, who went in and out in all the right places and was, understandably, much more attractive to Hugh's eye than the Bewhiskered One. He invited her to join us for lunch, and all chances of talking about my proposed move from the *Star* to the *Mirror* were lost as Hugh – later Lord Cudlipp – set about making an impression on the girl rather than me. He suddenly remembered a pressing appointment as we considered ordering a second bottle of bubbly, and dashed off with the parting shot, 'I'll call you next week.'

Two weeks went by, and no call. I dropped into a sulky 'well-I'm-not-going-to-call-you-if-you-won't-call-me' mood. When the telephone did eventually ring, the voice on the other end of the line said, 'Roy, Arthur Christiansen here. Have you a spare moment to pop up and see me at the *Express* office? The sooner the better.'

Christiansen – Chris, to all – was, in the view of those who know, the most gifted of all newspaper editors. Supported by Lord Beaverbrook's deep pocket, he had built the *Daily Express* into the leading middle-market broadsheet newspaper. To be summoned by him was a call from the top of the mountain. He told me that he was not going to let me leave his office until I had agreed to join the *Express*. His objective, he confided, was to have 'the Four Musketeers' of the cartooning world on the *Express* staff: Carl Giles, Osbert Lancaster, Michael Cummings and myself. Chris then mentioned the little matter of a £5,000-a-year contract, more than double what I was earning on *The Star*. Also thrown in as an extra enticement was a bright red, streamlined Ford Zephyr office car ('Oh, we've got a fire engine,' said six-year-old Freya when first seeing it). I was suddenly an *Express* man. Hugh Cudlipp was absolutely furious when he heard the news, and it was at least two years before he could bring himself to talk to me again. I felt as if the *Mirror* and *Express* had had a tug of war over my moustache.

Cudlipp got his way with Peter Wilson, whom he coaxed back from the *Express* to rejoin the *Mirror* in 1953. The main reason Peter made the return journey was that he could not stand the sight of *Express* sports editor Harold Hardman, a most morose man who, I have to admit, had a manner that made it very difficult for anybody to like him. He and Wilson used to sit back to back to each other in the *Express* sports department, and communicate through tersely written memos delivered by their secretaries.

I got 'ringside' knowledge of the tension between Wilson and Hardman when I was on my first overseas assignment for the *Star* in 1951. It was the return match between Randolph Turpin and Sugar Ray Robinson in New York, just sixty-four days after Turpin had caused a major upset by relieving Robinson of his world middleweight title with a fifteen rounds points victory on a Jack Solomons promotion at Earls Court. I flew from Dublin in a giant B.O.A.C. Stratacruiser in which I had a sleeping berth. The air fare was £300, which made quite a hole in the limited *Star* budget.

Wilson, reporting for the *Express*, was one of the leading Fleet Street authorities on lawn tennis, and sent back a story from New York about a new rising sixteen-year-old star he had just seen called Maureen 'Little Mo' Connolly. Back came a cable from Hardman in the *Express* office: ALL I WANT FROM YOU IS BOXING BOXING BOXING.

Wilson, who had gone to the tennis because both Robinson and Turpin had taken a day off from training, sent back this cabled response: REGRET NEITHER MAN WORKING WORKING WORKING TODAY TODAY TODAY STOP REGARDS REGARDS REGARDS WILSON WILSON WILSON.

Turpin got himself in some bother with a girl in New York, and gave promoter Jack 'King' Solomons (left) all sorts of problems in the build-up to the fight. The trouble hit the headlines in the American newspapers, and Jack decided to drive out to the Grossingers training camp to see Turpin and calm him down. He hired a Cadillac and invited me to join him for the drive. It was getting late and in a bid to get to the training camp before dark, Jack put his foot down

These were among my ringside drawings from New York when I reported as well as cartooned!

Robinson, above, had Turpin helpless on the ropes in the final seconds of the tenth round.

too heavily on the accelerator. A patrolman chased us, and in those days if you were caught speeding after dark you had to report immediately to a local night court. When the Judge asked Solomons what he was doing in the United States, Jack explained that he was Turpin's promoter. 'Mister,' said the Judge, 'you've got enough problems. Case dismissed!'

The following week Turpin was stopped by Robinson in the last seconds of the tenth round after being on the verge of another victory over Sugar Ray, who was badly cut over the left eye. I not only drew my impressions of the fight, but also reported it. The *Star* could not afford the luxury of sending two staffmen to New York. What with cabling my eyewitness account of the fight back to London and also wireless-wiring my instant cartoon of the action via the ionosphere, I felt in need of rescuing by the referee long before the tenth round.

There was a lot of controversy over referee Ruby Goldstein's decision to stop the fight with Turpin under a two-fisted attack on the ropes. Years later Ruby told me, 'We could not afford another fatality. I was too aware that just days before Georgie Flores had died after taking a beating in the ring. I was not going to have Turpin's death on my conscience.' A hard, hard game, boxing.

While in New York for the fight, I met up with a fellow cartoonist called

65

Ham Fisher, the American famous for his world-wide syndicated Joe Palooka strip. We cartooned each other while having a meal together, and Ham's instant

pencilled vision of me appears on the left along with his Palooka character.

I never got around to having my work syndicated. It was very British oriented, and it would not really have travelled well. I was never the world's greatest businessman, and I recently calculated that during my lifetime I have drawn several thousand cartoons for no financial reward. If only I had had Freya as my manager! But who cares about cash? As comedian Tommy Trinder once said to me, 'What good is happiness? It can't buy you money!'

Harold Hardman did not exactly welcome me with open arms when I joined his *Express* sports staff. I was an exclusive Arthur Christiansen appointment, and that rankled with him. I would not for one minute begin to even hint that he did it deliberately, but when I went on my first major assignment for the *Express* – the 1953 Grand National, won by Early Mist – he gave me a measurement for my cartoon that was all wrong. When the cartoon arrived at the office it had to be stretched to fit the hole left for it, and everything was pulled out of alignment. *Express* readers must have felt their new sports cartoonist was a drunk.

I had an early run-in with Hardman when he gave my Press Box ticket for a Lord's Test to features columnist Nancy Spain. It was a trial of strength as to what I would be prepared to take from Mr Hardman. Anybody will tell you that I am the most easy-going person walking this earth. In fact I am so laid back at times that people have often pronounced me dead. But on this occasion I decided to come out fighting. I went and saw Chris, who recovered the ticket for me because he felt that I should have the Press Box view. It all seems pretty childish from this distance, but pecking order is all important in newspaper offices.

Hardman did not like the fact that the Editor and I were social friends. Chris came down to Essex for a game of golf and when I introduced him to Maggie he said, 'Well, what do you think of your Roy joining the *Express*?'

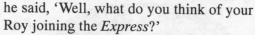

CHRIS WAS MORE EXCAVATOR THAN GOLFER

Maggie gave him a withering look, and said, 'What do YOU think of the *Express* being lucky enough to get my Roy?'

It was one of the few times in his life when Chris was speechless. From then on he treated Maggie with a lot of love and affection, and a little caution. Nobody messes with my lovely Maggie.

Chris decided to bill me as 'Britain's Greatest Sports Cartoonist', and the publicity department swamped the country with posters of a self-portrait.

It is the one that introduces each chapter of this book, only it was blown up to twice the size of my head. I thought it looked pretty awful with my moustache spreading across the page like a huge hedge, and so I added a sparrow to give it a lift. The sparrow and I became quite inseparable, and he was for many years a resident lodger in my cartoons (even accompanying me to Royal Ascot, right!).

Lord Beaverbrook was advised of my arrival at the *Express*, and I was invited to lunch with the leading press baron of Fleet Street. This was when he famously told me in his Canadian accent that I would not become a millionaire working for him, but that I would live like one!

I certainly did that when in the company of the man who took over as the flamboyant *Express* columnist, Desmond Hackett. He was one of Fleet Street's unforgettable entertainers, who first coined the phrase: 'Don't let facts spoil a good story'. Des and I travelled the world together, and he used to introduce me to people as, 'his Lordship'. He pretended that I was a British earl, travelling incognito, and that he was my private secretary. Our double act used to go down particularly well in the United States, where we were often wined and dined on the strength of my nonexistent aristocratic background. On one occasion in Chicago, *Daily Mail* boxing reporter Jack Wood joined Des in convincing the promoters of the Chicago Meat Fair that I was

Lord Smithfield, of London's famous Smithfield meat market. Des, Jack and I were made guests of honour at the top table at their banquet. I made a speech strengthening anglo-American relations, and we all got as drunk as lords.

Those were the days of yelling your copy into a telephone and hoping that

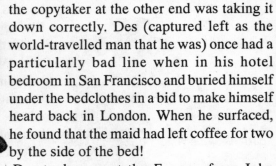

the copytaker at the other end was taking it down correctly. Des (captured left as the world-travelled man that he was) once had a particularly bad line when in his hotel bedroom in San Francisco and buried himself under the bedclothes in a bid to make himself heard back in London. When he surfaced, he found that the maid had left coffee for two by the side of the bed!

Des took over at the *Express* from John Macadam, a wonderfully gifted Scot who was more essayist than sports writer. John, who had a moustache to rival mine and an artistic and theatrical background, once wrote of a dull, uneventful goalless draw at Millwall: 'This was Much Ado about Nothing Nothing'.

A tinkering sub-editor changed it to, 'This was Much Ado about Nil Nil'.

John used to invite, Maggie, Freya and myself down to his Cornwall cottage that was in Temperance Street. He was an imbiber on a grand scale, and called the cottage Hangover House! In those pre-breathalyser days, John – along with the likes of Peter Wilson, Des Hackett, Tom Phillips of the *Daily Herald* and Geoffrey Green, of *The Times* – could have drunk for Britain. They were big drinkers, big men and big talents.

It was a great day for all of us on the *Express* when Hardman the Hard Man made way for a friendly, creative Scottish sports editor called Bob Findlay. He was an inspirational character, except when it came to picking horse racing winners, and he was like a breath of fresh air blowing through the sports department. It was under Bob's stewardship that Des and I first became a regular team following the saddest day I ever knew in Fleet Street. This was 6 February 1958, the day of the terrible Munich air crash. Eight leading players of the Manchester United team and three club officials were among the twenty-three who perished when their charter plane crashed on take off after a refuelling stop in Munich on the way back from a European Cup tie in Belgrade. That was tragic enough. What made it even harder for us in the newspaper industry to

Munich, 1958. If a picture speaks a thousand words, then a cartoon should speak one thousand and one.

The 1958 FA Cup Final was played in the shadow of the Munich tragedy, and the sentiments and support of the nation outside Bolton were with Matt Busby and his hastily rebuilt Manchester United team. Matt came out of hospital in time to see the match, but two-goal Nat Lofthouse ruined any chance of a fairy story victory.

70

take was that among the dead were eight journalists: Alf Clarke *(Manchester Evening Chronicle)*, Don Davies *(Manchester Guardian)*, George Follows *(Daily Herald)*, Tom Jackson *(Manchester Evening News)*, Archie Ledbrooke *(Daily Mirror)*, Eric Thompson *(Daily Mail)*, former England goalkeeper Frank Swift *(News of the World)* and our chief northern *Daily Express* sports columnist Henry Rose. Dear Henry was based in Manchester and was the Voice of Sport in the North. He could sway opinions with his hard-hitting articles, and had a pen that could grill or glorify according to the view that he wanted to put across. An indication of his standing in the north is that on the day of his funeral Manchester taxi drivers waived all fares as they ferried journalists to and from the cemetery.

Henry was unmatchable, but in Des the *Express* had somebody who was equally equipped with the sort of outrageous opinions that could make readers sit up and take notice. Hackett, the Man in the Brown Bowler, was a born showman, and used to make crazy predictions to force reactions from readers. Des once wrote that if Chelsea reached the FA Cup Final he would walk barefoot to Wembley. Chelsea duly battled through to the Final against Spurs in 1967.

As Des – never one to duck his duty (particularly when he knew its circulation value) – started on his barefoot walk, he was accompanied by manager Tommy Docherty and half a dozen Chelsea first-team players, who were ribbing him in good-humoured style. A council rubbish truck came slowly by and Des, without breaking step, said to the Chelsea players, 'Here you are, chaps, your coach has arrived to take you to Wembley.'

Tommy Doc, not exactly slow with the quips, applauded. 'That's Des,' he said, 'the king of the instant one-liners.'

What Des did not know is that one of the Chelsea players had put his shoes on to the rubbish truck. Happy days.

Geoffrey Green was another eccentric character who filled Fleet Street with his presence. An idea of Geoffrey's extrovert personality can be gleaned from the fact that when a leg injury necessitated the use of a crutch he attended an England international match at Wembley Stadium with a stuffed parrot sitting on his shoulder! Cambridge-

Tommy Docherty

educated Green was an intellectual who could have made a career for himself as a lawyer. But he preferred the press box and the drinks bar to the courtroom and the legal bar.

I spent many enjoyable hours in Geoffrey's company, and one story that stands out in my memory is of when, during an England tour match in Poland, he and Laurie Pignon (then on the *Daily Sketch*) were arrested for causing a disturbance in the city centre of Katowice. This was in the pre-Solidarity days, and Geoffrey

71

was making a public speech about the values of a free society. Laurie, the absolute epitome of the 'terribly English' gentleman, who had been given a rough time as a prisoner-of-war in Poland, was seconding Geoffrey's argument.

Two guards, in ankle-length fur-lined coats, appeared from out of nowhere and marched Geoffrey and Laurie away. A few hours later, with their worried press colleagues on the point of calling in the British ambassador, they reappeared wearing broad, drunken grins and, would you believe, a fur lined, ankle-length guardsman's coat each! Geoffrey continued to wear his coveted coat in the press boxes of the world right up until his retirement as the man from *The Times*. I don't think lovable Laurie Pignon would have considered wearing his coat in the Wimbledon press box in his role as the distinguished lawn-tennis correspondent for the *Daily Mail*.

Geoffrey had a habit of using song-lines when he talked, and he always greeted people with phrases like 'Younger than springtime ...' or 'Over the rainbow, baby ...'

When Bobby Moore arrived at Mexico Airport after his arrest in Bogota on a trumped-up jewel theft charge before the 1970 World Cup finals, Geoffrey was in the throng of pressmen waiting on the Tarmac at the bottom of the plane disembarkment steps. As Bobby stood on the top step, illuminated by scores of flashing camera light bulbs, he looked down and spotted Geoffrey. He punched a fist into the air and shouted, 'Over the rainbow, baby!' Foreign reporters, anxious to record Bobby's first words on his return to freedom, scratched their heads as they tried to decipher just what the England captain had said.

Ah, Bobby Moore ... Geoffrey Green ... Desmond Hackett. They don't make them like that any more. They were giants among men and brought light and laughter to my sixty years in Fleet Street.

I know that my memory is not deceiving me when I say that the sportswriters back then were greater characters than you get now. This was before sport kowtowed to the great god of television, and the likes of Wilson, Hackett, Green, Pignon, J.L. Manning, E.W. Swanton, Peter O'Sullevan, Clive Graham, George Whiting and Donald Saunders were revered (and occasionally reviled) for their opinions. The march of television started to erode their authority, particularly an entertainer like Des who used to write for effect. His colourful descriptive writing was suddenly exposed as owing a lot to his imagination as the television camera revealed what *really* happened. For Des, and for readers, a lot of the fun started to go out of the reporting business.

Thankfully, the television camera could not yet present sport in cartoon form, and I continued happily to capture the often funny, sometimes sad but always fascinating face of sport.

Now for a cartoon cavalcade of sports celebrities who made the fifties come alive for me and my pencil ...

THE WIZARD OF DRIBBLE MAKES THE BALL SIT UP AND TALK, AND BOLTON ARE LOST FOR WORDS

Stanley Matthews ran Bolton's defence dizzy in the 1953 FA Cup final. It became known as the Matthews Final after Blackpool had come from behind to win 4-3. But it would be better remembered as the Stanleys Final, because his team-mate Stan Mortensen scored the only hat-trick in an FA Cup final at Wembley.

A brace of Baileys kept my pen busy in the 1950s. Emmanuel McDonald Bailey (left) was Britain's outstanding sprinter in the immediate post-war years and won fourteen successive AAA sprint titles over 100 and 220 yards. He collected a bronze medal in the 100 metres final in the 1952 Helsinki Olympics, clocking the same time as the winner. He was nicknamed the Black Flash. There could not have been a greater contrast between two sportsmen than between McDonald Bailey and Barnacle Bailey.

Trevor Bailey has been a friend and neighbour of mine for more than fifty years, but that has not stopped me lampooning some of his snail-pace, snore-inducing batting performances. But for all my joking at Trevor's expense, I happen to think he has been one of English cricket's greatest heroes. He had a heart bigger than his head, and when we regained the Ashes in 1953 he was one of the men of the series with stubborn batting that broke the spirit of the Australian bowlers.

SPIN MASTER JIM LAKER HAS THE AUSSIE 'ROOS ON THE HOP

Jim Laker's 19 for 90 return against Australia at Old Trafford in 1956 is a Test record that is unlikely ever to be equalled, let alone beaten. The humbled Australians muttered angrily about the pitch being doctored to suit England's spin, yet Laker's spin 'twin' Tony Lock could manage only one wicket in the match despite bowling one more than Laker's 68 overs. The Australians were well and truly Lakered.

75

Chris Brasher was first across the line in the 1956 Olympic 3,000 metres steeplechase final, but was disqualified for allegedly jostling a rival at the water jump. Brasher appealed, and he was reinstated as gold medallist after an agonising wait. My Express colleague Des Hackett plied Chris with champagne while he was waiting for the result of the appeal, and by the time he got on the rostrum he was seeing double!

The 1956 Olympic Games in Melbourne were memorable for the gold medal performances of boxers Dick McTaggart and Terry Spinks, and swimmer Judy Grinham.

Irate Birmingham City supporters threatened to march on the Express office after I had depicted their players as animals before the 1956 FA Cup final against Manchester City (above). Their calls for my head inspired the cartoon on the right. The Birmingham players saw the funny side of it, and asked for the original for their dressing-room.

77

Sports cartooning is not always a funny business. I often used my platform in the Express *to make a serious point. I was, for instance, concerned after British bulldog Don Cockell had taken a terrible hiding from Rocky Marciano in a savage world heavyweight title fight in San Francisco in 1955. Don eventually took the advice to hang up his gloves, but he rarely enjoyed good health after a nine round beating that no man should have been allowed to take. Don, too brave for his own good, had warned his corner not to stop the contest regardless of what happened. They should have ignored him.*

Len Hutton knew when to hang up his batting gloves. He declared his great innings in 1955 after a 79-Test career in which he scored 6071 runs at an average 56.67. The first professional to captain England in modern cricket, he was knighted for his services to the game in 1956.

Henry Cooper and his manager Jim 'The Bishop' Wicks were great friends of mine. I loved the way Jim always talked in the royal 'we'... unless Henry had lost. Then he would switch to, 'Our Enery'.

'Enery, if we want to be World Champ and switch the lights on at Morecambe, we'd better put this geyser's out at Porthcawl tonight...

WITH BEST WISHES TO HENRY COOPER WHO IS REPRESENTING HIS MANAGER JIM WICKS IN THE RING TONIGHT AGAINST GAWIE DE KLERK FOR THE EMPIRE HEAVYWEIGHT CHAMPIONSHIP.

Lester Piggott on CREPELLO in the King George VI and Queen Elizabeth Stakes

Aintree Grand Prix STIRLING MOSS TONY BROOKS and LEWIS EVANS

Derek Ibbotson in the White City "MILE IN A MILLION"

Four Legs, Four Wheels and a Pair of Heels! WHAT PRICE THEIR BRINGING OFF A TREBLE FOR GREAT BRITAIN?

It was the Daily Express *that pioneered Sportsman of the Year awards, an idea taken up by BBC TV when they realised how popular the idea was. My nominations for the 1957 award, featured in the cartoon on the left, led by mile record holder Derek Ibbotson and Lester Piggott, winner of the Derby on Crepello.*

Prince Philip liked this cartoon so much that he asked for the original. It shows the Prince meeting American light-heavyweight Jimmy Slade in the ring at Harringay Arena before his 1950s fight against Don Cockell. The Jack Solomons promotion was staged in aid of the National Playing Fields Association.

5: The Ali and Alf Years

MUHAMMAD ALI IS TICKLED BY
MY MOUSTACHE, I MEET THE
BEATLES, TAKE THE FULL WEIGHT
OF COLIN MILBURN'S HUMOUR, AND
DRAW A LOT OF SATISFACTION
FROM ARNIE AND ALF'S ARMIES.

THE swinging sixties were a God-send to sports cartoonists. Everywhere that I pointed my pencil, there was a great character waiting to be portrayed, pilloried, parodied and/or praised. Bless them all, I say, from the spouting Muhammad Ali to the sporting Bobby Charlton, from the England express Fred Trueman to the expressionless Alf Ramsey, from the polished Pele to the posteriorly challenged Colin Cowdrey, from the poleaxe-punching Henry Cooper to the post-passing Lester Piggott, from the menacing Sonny Liston to the mesmerising Mary Rand, and from the ruthless Arnold Palmer to the toothless Nobby Stiles.

Climb with me aboard my time machine and come back to meet these sporting icons who took so much lead from my pencil that it is a wonder I did not run dry. First stop, Rome. It's the 1960 Olympics, and a young eighteen-year-old American light-heavyweight is making so much noise in the Olympic village that we cannot avoid him. His name, he tells the world, is Cassius Marcellus Clay.

I immediately dubbed him Gaseous Cassius. 'I am The Greatest,' he says. It is to become his anthem throughout the sixties, through the seventies and, sadly, into the eighties when he went several fights too far. He changed his name, but not his act. Muhammad Ali became a magnet for the world's media as he danced like a butterfly, stung like a bee, shuffled and showboated and provided exciting action to go with his words. He was, without doubt, one of the greatest showmen of the 20th century, whose fame transcended sport and whose face (and voice) became the most widely recognised throughout the world.

Ali always seemed transfixed by my moustache as we came face to face in places as far apart as Rome, Los Angeles, Houston, Miami and London during his globe-trotting career.

'Man,' he said during training for the fight in which he relieved Sonny Liston of the world title, 'is that mustash for real? Or is it one of them joke tashes? You sure you're not a Liston spy in disguise, 'cos if you are you can tell that big, bad,

Ringside point of view.
ALAS! WRONG 'AMMER!

British heavyweight hero Henry Cooper challenged Muhammad Ali for the world title at Highbury in 1966. Sadly, as in their first fight three years earlier, Our Enery's flesh let him down. He was stopped with a cut eye in the sixth round.

Muhammad Ali was a target for my pencil for more than twenty years. This was how I portrayed him when he first became king of the world heavyweights following his stunning victory over sullen Sonny Liston in Miami in 1964.

82

ugly bear that I'm gonna give him such a whupping that his ma and pa won't recognise him.'

When he came to London to fight Our 'Enery Cooper at Wembley, he stopped a sparring session to tell me, 'I see you've still got your joke mustash. Man, with a mustash like that you could fly without a plane.'

Ali used to greet me with, 'Here comes the Very English Mustash.' He would peep over my shoulder while I was drawing and say, 'Wish I could draw like that. It's easier painting faces than trying to punch them, and them drawings don't hit back!'

I fascinated him once by telling him that former world heavyweight champion Primo Carnera had been a good artist. I had met the Ambling Alp on a couple of his visits to London, and he used to take a deep interest in my work, and he showed me some of his portrait and landscape paintings. It was good enough to suggest that had he given all his attention to it he could have become a fine artist. Ali considered the facts, and then shut me up with the comment: 'Well, Mustash, I would rather be a great artist on canvas in the ring.'

Most times I saw Ali in action I used to come away after his fights sharing his opinion that he truly was The Greatest. But I also saw him sink to gutter level with his tactics against Ernie Terrell, when he cruelly and continually taunted and tormented his opponent. 'What's ma name?' he kept asking the outgunned Terrell, who had insisted on referring to him as Cassius Clay in the build-up to the fight.

Ali punched Terrell to the point of unconsciousness several times in the fight, and then deliberately pulled back to prolong the agony. It was a pity rather than pretty to watch, and I conveyed my feelings in a cartoon that questioned Ali's sportsmanship.

Ali was not pleased with me, particularly as I referred to him as Clay. But, as I said at the time: 'You have to draw the line somewhere, oh Great One.'

The cartoon that upset Clay ... sorry, Ali

I was ringside at Wembley Stadium the night Henry Cooper – 'Our 'Enery' – landed the left hook that dumped Ali, or Clay as he was then known, on the seat of his pants. He was wobbly legged and glassy eyed as he pulled himself up as the bell rang to save him at the end of the fourth round. Then trainer Angelo Dundee won extra time for Clay to recover when he reported to the referee that one of his gloves had split. I would never accuse the angelic Angelo of cheating, but there were suspicions that he had deliberately cut the glove with his scissors. Just as the bell rang for the start of the fifth round, a great ball of horsehair flew out of the ring from the direction of Clay's corner and landed between the typewriters being pounded by Des Hackett and Peter Wilson. Des put it in his raincoat pocket, and later produced it as evidence that it was more than just a tear in Clay's glove.

Poor Henry was stopped in the fifth round with a terrible cut eye that pumped blood. His spirit was always willing, but his flesh was weak and continually let him down in major fights. Henry's manager Jim 'The Bishop' Wicks, who always spoke in the royal 'we', said: 'We was within a whisker of causing the upset of the century.' Jim was very protective of Our 'Enery, and when it was suggested that he could challenge world champion Sonny Liston – then considered the most dangerous fighter on the planet – he retorted: 'We do not even want to be in the same room as Mr Liston, let alone the same ring.'

Ali had no such fears of sharing the ring with Liston, and shocked the world by taking the title when Liston quit on his stool with a damaged shoulder after six rounds of a one-sided fight at Miami Beach in 1964. From my ringside seat,

ALI OOPS! SONNY MISSES AGAIN

This was one of my instant ringside drawings during the first Ali-Liston fight at Miami Beach in 1964. Poor old Sonny kept hitting and missing as Clay danced like a butterfly and stung like a bee.

I formed the strong view that Liston was suffering more from a damaged heart than a damaged shoulder. He had been totally outfought, and out-thought by his brash and flash young challenger, who was only in trouble in the fifth round when he complained of having been blinded by a substance rubbed on to Liston's gloves. It certainly was not knockout drops because the lumbering Liston was unable to get close enough to him to deliver any of the bombs that had twice flattened Floyd Patterson in one round.

The promoters pulled off quite

WE LOVE ALI, YEAH, YEAH, YEAH

BEATLES Paul, Ringo, George and John

a publicity coup during the build-up to the fight when they got the Beatles, John, Paul, George and Ringo, to visit Ali at his training camp. The four mop-heads, who were then the hottest property in the pop music world, all lay prostrate in the ring at his feet. He was the only man in the world who could claim to be a bigger noise than them! John Lennon took a closer interest in my cartooning than in meeting Ali ('Don't quote me,' he said, 'but I find boxing barbaric.') He said that his hobby was sketching, and that if it had not been for his music he would have liked to have tried making a living as a cartoonist. In later years, of course, he had a lot of his drawings published. As with his music, he had an individual flair that would have earned him popularity with his pencil.

The second Ali-Liston fight in Lewiston, Maine, was a real stinkeroo. Liston went down and out to a first round phantom punch that nobody saw, certainly not old Sonny. All hell broke loose, and my head was trampled on as police tried to cordon off the ring from protesting fans. I finished my work hiding under the ring canvas, clinging on to my precious bottle of ink.

Ali put it about later that the knockout punch had come to him from the grave. He claimed he had a visitation from an old fighter from the past, who showed him how to deliver the blow. Ali has Irish blood somewhere deep in his veins, and I can only describe his claim as a lot of old blarney. I was next to ringside commentator Eamonn Andrews, who was the first to reach Ali for his view of the brief encounter. As Ali prepared for his interview he was saying to his handlers, 'What was the punch ... quick, what put him down?' Like everybody else, he did not have a clue.

I felt sorry for old Sonny, whose name hardly conveyed his sullen outlook on life. Hardly anybody liked Liston, and the ex-convict always looked as if the world was on his shoulders. Mind you, I did once see him laugh so much that he fell off his chair. It was at a press conference before his first brutal demolition of Floyd 'Freud' Patterson in Chicago. For some reason he commented on the fact that black men have fewer hairs on their legs than white men.

86

The effervescent Reg Gutteridge, reporting the fight for the London *Evening News*, said, 'Well, I'll bet you ten bucks you've got more hair on your legs than me.' Liston, a born gambler, could not resist, and challenged Reg to roll up his trouser leg ready for a hair count. What Reg had not told him is that he had lost a leg when treading on a mine during the D-Day landings in Normandy. When Sonny saw the hairless false leg, he just keeled over laughing uncontrollably. I think it was the only time I ever saw him obviously enjoying himself.

I will return to Muhammad Ali in a later chapter, but I want us to briefly go back to Rome where I first met him during the 1960 Olympics. The *Express* sent a team of four reporters, myself along with Des Hackett, Sydney Hulls (son of the top pre-war boxing promoter of the same name) and 1956 Olympic swimming gold medallist Judy Grinham. We were each presented with an Italian scooter to get around town, and were photographed for publicity purposes on a scooter tour. What the photos did not show was Judy Grinham falling off the back of my scooter. Thankfully, Judy was unhurt and I was able to tell her: 'You're obviously a swimmer not a diver. That was a very low tariff dive.'

Next to Ali, it was England football manager Alf Ramsey who provided me with most material throughout much of the sixties. Alf had a wonderful, full-of-character face that was easy to draw because it did not change expression, regardless of what was happening out on the pitch. He remained sphinx-like even when England won the 1966 World Cup final at Wembley and always kept his composure – apart from after the quarter-final with Argentina. As England defender George Cohen attempted to swap shirts with an Argentine player, Alf raced between them and dragged the England shirt back. 'We don't give our shirts to these bloody animals,' he raged. When he repeated the 'animals' description at the press conference, it caused a diplomatic incident between England and Argentina. I thought Alf should have issued an immediate apology ... to animals everywhere, and I conveyed this feeling in the *Express* with the cartoon on the facing page. It was the only time I got any feedback from Alf, who told his right-hand man Harold Shepherdson: 'I would apologise to the animals before I say sorry to the Argentinians!'

My cartoon of Alf remaining expressionless throughout a match (also on the facing page) appealed so much to his former Ipswich Town chairman John Cobbold that he asked for the original to be framed and he hung it in the Ipswich boardroom. 'You have captured dear Alf perfectly,' he told me. 'You could have put a fire under his seat, and he would have looked his same calm, immovable self. The description "imperturbable" could have been created for Alf.'

Ramsey gave every impression of hating foreigners, and this to him included Scots. Des Hackett and I were on a train journey with Alf returning from an international at Hampden that England had won. A Scottish fan pulled open the door to the first-class compartment and said, 'I would just like you to know that

I thought you were lucky as hell to win today.' Happy to have delivered his message, the Scot walked off down the corridor. Alf got up and opened the door. 'Excuse me,' he said with his forced plummy English voice, and politely beckoned to the Scot to come back. When he was within a yard or so, Alf briefly went back to his East of London roots and hissed, 'Why don't you piss off.' He then returned to his seat as if nothing had happened.

For another match against Scotland in Glasgow, Alf arrived by plane and was greeted at the airport by a Scottish journalist who said, 'Welcome to Scotland.' Alf fixed him with his famous cold-eyed stare and replied, 'You must be f—joking.'

One of the secrets of Ramsey's success was his fierce loyalty to his players. When the Toothless Tiger Nobby Stiles was kicking lumps out of the opposition during the 1966 World Cup finals, Alf was advised by senior officials that he should drop the Manchester United ball winner. 'If Stiles goes, I go,' was Alf's terse response. The officials backed off. Thank goodness for that! Nobby was a gift to sports cartoonists with his gummy snarl, spindly legs and fierce competitive attitude. Off the pitch, he was as sweet as a pussy cat, but once he crossed the white line on behalf of England or Manchester United he became a tiger. A toothless tiger, of course, because he always used to leave his false teeth in the dressing-room. He was not exactly the prettiest sight without his teeth, and a Liverpool fan once began a letter to him, 'Dear Ugly'.

Nobby always left his teeth in the dressing room.

Two years after the World Cup triumph, nobbly Nobby was back in my sights as the midfield terrier in United's 1968 European Cup final triumph against Benfica at Wembley. He was charged with the job of keeping the Black Panther Eusebio under lock and key, a job that he did coldly and calculatingly – just as he had done when England played Portugal in the 1966 World Cup semi-final. That was when the Portuguese pleaded with the referee to protect the Panther from the Tiger!

The 1968 European Cup final belonged, of course, to manager Matt Busby and his

Nobbly Nobby, the Toothless Tiger marvellous skipper Bobby Charlton, both

Three of the Manchester United giants of the 1960s. Above: Matt Busby, whose dream of the European Cup finally came true at Wembley in 1968, ten years after surviving the Munich air crash. Nobby Stiles (above, right) played a vital role in the victory over Benfica by keeping quiet the Portuguese Black Panther, Eusebio. Bobby Charlton scored two goals in the European Cup final, and two seasons later won the 100th of his 106 England caps. He, too, was a Munich survivor, and – like Sir Matt – went on to earn a knighthood.

Arnie Palmer retained the British Open title at Troon in 1962 despite the handicap of a strained muscle. Australian Kel Nagle was six shots away in second place.

of whom had survived the Munich air crash ten years earlier. Charlton, along with George Best and Denis Law, made United the most exciting team of the sixties, and a joy to watch for a scribbler like me. I was very fond of Matt, who was a gentleman of the first order. He would often telephone to thank me for featuring him in one of my cartoons, and regularly used to ask for the original. His parting shot whenever we met was always, 'May your whiskers never droop!'

Golf occupied much of my time in the 1960s, both playing and watching the masters in action. The decade started with Arnold Palmer crushing all comers with two successive Open triumphs, and ended with Tony Jacklin restoring English golfing pride by holding both the British and United States Open at the same time.

Arnie Palmer was the man who turned golf from a quaint, almost quirky way of making a living into a sport that grabbed the attention of the mass media.

Motivated by the emergence of Gary Player and Jack Nicklaus, Palmer more than anybody transformed golf into a major sport. He had an electric personality, and always played an attacking game that thrilled his huge galleries that became known as 'Arnie's Army'. I used to follow Arnie around the course because he was a certainty to provide cartooning material.

I will never forget his miraculous shot at the 16th at Royal Birkdale in the final round on his way to the first of his British Open titles. He had pushed his tee-shot into heavy rough. Most of us would have needed a mechanical digger to get the ball out on to the fairway. Arnie took a six iron and thrashed through the knee-deep rough with astonishing strength. The ground almost shook with the power, and he uprooted a small bush as the ball came soaring up. We were astonished to see the ball

Tony Jacklin, putting British golf on top

91

land on the green 140 yards away. It was such an amazing shot that a plaque now marks the spot where Arnie struck.

Tony 'Jacko' Jacklin became a good friend of the *Express* sports team. He was a regular visitor to our Fleet Street office, and was a particularly close pal of our sports editor John Morgan, a creative journalist who had taken over the hot seat from Bob Findlay. John, who came from my neck of the woods in Essex, kept insisting that Jacko was going to become the first British-born Open winner since Max Faulkner back in 1951. We almost drowned in champagne when he played out of his skin to win the Open at Royal Lytham & St Anne's in 1969. I asked him what it was like to walk to the final green knowing that he was a putt away from becoming Open champion. 'I was absolutely petrified,' he said. 'Jack Nicklaus was one of the first to congratulate me, and I said, "God, Jack, I never knew anybody could be so scared on a golf course." Nicklaus replied, "Fear is the greatest motivator of all. We must learn to feed off it."'

It was like being close to a lottery winner to see the change to Jacko's life. His fee for an exhibition game suddenly jumped from £150 to £3000. He was in demand to endorse golf shoes, clubs, gloves, airlines, socks, hats, even whisky.

A record company paid him to make a Sinatra-style album, and, of course, he had an instructional strip and column in the *Express*, where we all felt part of his success. John Morgan was particularly pleased. He had backed him at long odds while most of the experts were laughing at his prediction that Jacko was going to beat the likes of Nicklaus, Gary Player and Lee Trevino. Whacko Jacko!

My golfing exploits were more modest. I played in the Bowmaker Pro-am tournament at Sunningdale with the South African golfing genius Bobby Locke and horror film star Christopher Lee, a scratch golfer and certainly no sucker on the golf course. There was generous applause when I hit my tee shot at one of the short holes on the homeward half to within a foot of the flag. I was feeling pleased with myself until I heard a spectator comment for the entire gallery to hear: 'It's about time he bloody hit a decent shot.'

One of my opponents in another pro-am was comedian Charlie Drake, who was a mean little competitor. It is customary in these sort of charity affairs to 'give' your opponent any putt under two feet. I put the ball to within eighteen inches of the hole, and then I waited for Charlie to nod that it was okay for me to pick up. He studied where my ball lay, and then said: 'There's still a lot of golf left in that.'

I was so shocked that I nearly missed the putt.

On the cricket front, my pen was well served by two great England stalwarts Fred Trueman and Colin Cowdrey. Fiery Fred featured so many times in my cartoons that he told my father-in-law, a near neighbour up in his native Yorkshire, 'I dare not retire. I'm keeping that f— son-in-law of yours in work.'

Charming Colin Cowdrey took my, uh, full frontal assaults on his backside with bottomless good spirit, and was happy to take a back seat – so to speak – when that larger-than-life character Colin Milburn joined him in the England team. The two Colins were colossal, both in talent and bulk. I portrayed them together at the wicket blocking out the sun, and Olly Milburn, a really lovely man with a sharp Geordie wit, wrote to me asking

Fiery Fred, my dear pen pal

93

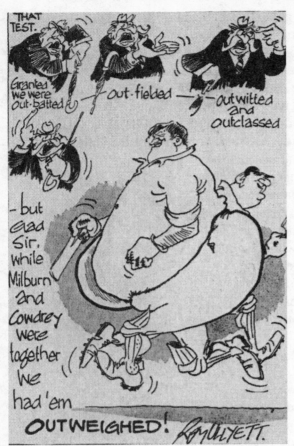

The two Colins, Cowdrey and Milburn, gave me tons of ammunition. They were a couple of swells. As much as I poked fun at Cowdrey and Fred Trueman, I was a great admirer of their cricketing ability. They were both into the autumn of their exceptional Test careers when another outstanding character and cartoonist's friend was just starting out (see below). Welcome Geoff Boycott in his bespectacled days.

Even when Fred retired, he could not escape my pencil. I followed him into the nightclubs and captured his stand up comedy act. He had a great delivery.

for the original. He added a heart-felt postscript: 'I hope you grow fat!'

Ollie's weight used to balloon, and his Northants captain Keith Andrew saw him sinking a pint in the pavilion bar. 'Olly,' he pleaded, 'for goodness sake stick to halves.'

'Okay, skipper,' said Olly, who then turned to the barman and said: 'Two halves, please.'

It was tragic when Olly lost an eye in a car smash, but he never lost his sense of humour. The last time I saw him, before his sad death at the age of 48, I asked after his health. 'Oh, I'm fine,' he said. 'It only hurts when I walk.' He then let out a huge laugh, and ordered a pint. A light went out when Olly departed to the great pavilion in the sky.

I always tried not to let my gentle lampooning cross the cruelty border. There is a fine line where humour ends and humiliation starts. I think I must have got close to it with my cartoons of boxing promoter Harry Levene. I was always pointing up the state of war that existed between Harry and his deadly rival Jack Solomons. They had a genuine, blowtorch hatred for each other. Both were my friends, and I used to try unsuccessfully to make the peace between them.

Harry had a rather prominent nose that was a compelling target for my pencil. It got to the point where I was comparing it to Concorde.

Jack 'King' Solomons v Harry 'The Hooter' Levene.

He used to join Des Hacket, John Morgan and myself for regular liquid lunches, and would gush over my cartoons. I think Harry had more originals framed and hanging in his home than any other of my 'victims'. 'All publicity is good publicity,' Harry used to say.

One evening I was watching him being interviewed on television – I think it was by Harry Carpenter – when he was asked what he thought of my cartoon portrayal of his nose. I waited for Harry's usual 'all publicity is good publicity' response, and nearly spilled my Horlicks when he said, 'That man Roy Ullyett is ruining my love life.'

Des Hackett and I made many cross-Atlantic trips during the 1960s, usually to keep our eyes on the world heavyweight boxing scene. We were ringside for the three-fight serial between Floyd Patterson and the Swedebasher Ingemar Johansson, and again when Patterson was twice bludgeoned to first-round defeats by Sonny Liston. Patterson was so ridden with guilt by his performance in the first fight in Chicago that he left the stadium by a back exit, wearing a false beard and glasses so that nobody would recognise him. He really looked the part of 'Freud' Patterson. There was a bizarre incident as he drove home at high speed, still wearing his disguise. He was pulled up by a traffic cop, who asked for his driving licence. Patterson could not find it, and then sheepishly pulled down the beard to identify himself. The policeman scratched his head, and –

The sparrow flies me to New York (right) for the first Patterson-Johansson fight.

almost as embarrassed as Floyd – waved him on to continue his journey.

Johansson was one of the most unusual world champions to cross my path. He preferred night clubbing to training. When he arrived in New York to challenge Patterson for the world title he talked about his right hand as if it was something separate from the rest of his body. 'It is a gift from the Gods,' he said. 'It is mystic and moves faster than the eye can see. I do not tell it when to go. Suddenly, boom! It lands like toonder.' Ingo's Bingo was born.

I was very lucky to have so many great characters to draw in the 1960s. Here are just a few of them as captured by my pencil ...

Mary Bignal (above) was the pin-up girl of British sport for much of the 1960s. On the eve of winning her gold medal in the long jump in the 1964 Tokyo Olympics (as Mary Rand) she occupied herself by organising a bust-measuring contest in the British women's team headquarters. Quite a girl, our Mary. John Surtees was for several years the fastest thing on two and four wheels, and he remains the only man to have won world titles on a motor bike and in formula one racing. Ann Jones (right) was the first left-hander to win the women's singles at Wimbledon, beating Margaret Court in the 1969 semi-final and Billie-Jean King in the final. Ann was also a five-times world championship finalist as a table tennis player.

I tried hard to steer clear of politics, which I felt had no place in sport. I used to leave the political statements to my Express colleague of 40 years, Michael Cummings, who with one cleverly crafted cartoon could puncture the pomposity of any politician. But I was drawn in to the debate that raged in cricket about England's links with South Africa. The Reverend David Sheppard, now the Bishop of Liverpool, was a leading voice against playing the South Africans. I preferred it when he was making all the right noises with his bat as England's opening batsman.

Denis 'The Menace' Law was one of my favourite footballers of the 1960s. He had razor-sharp reflexes and could turn a half-chance into a goal in the blinking of an eye. I saw him in match-winning form for Scotland against England at Hampden Park in 1962. A year earlier at Wembley he was in the Scottish team hammered 9-3 by England.

Desmond Hackett was merciless on the Scots with his hard-hitting comments in the Express. *We used to take our lives in our hands on our regular visits to Glasgow for the Scotland-England matches. But instead of flattening Hackett and myself, the Scots used to give us the warmest of welcomes, and we could have swum home on the rivers of whisky they tried to pour down our throats. Here's tae ye, Jocks. You're the most hospitable people on earth.*

100

90 MINUTES FROM GLORY?

England!
England!
England!
England!
England!
England!
Engl...

THE NOT SO WHITE BALL?

The two faces of football in the sixties. We welcomed the winning face of Bobby Moore and the England team in the 1966 World Cup final. This was England's finest footballing hour. But three years earlier there was the unacceptable face when a betting scandal was exposed that led to several players, including England internationals Tony Kay and Peter Swan, being imprisoned. I thought a football wrapped in fivers conveyed the message.

101

Out of the Ring against Firpo

TOLEDO 1919. The crouching Manassa Mauler KO's WILLARD to become WORLD CHAMPION

LIVING IT OVER AGAIN WITH Jack Dempsey ON BROADWAY

The long count against Tunney cost him his crown

DEAR JACK, THANK YOU FOR THE DINNER AND FOR THE MEMORIES. AND, YES, YOU DO SERVE THE BEST STEAKS IN NEW YORK. AS THOUGH I WOULD DARE ARGUE WITH YOU. THEY SAY THE LAST THING A CHAMPION LOSES IS HIS PUNCH. YOURS IN SPORT, ROY ULLYETT

I had a wonderful three-hour journey down the boxing memory lane with Jack Dempsey during a visit to his New York Broadway restaurant in 1962. The old Manassa Mauler, arguably the hardest-hitting of all the world heavyweight champions, told me: 'At my peak, I would have closed Clay's mouth inside a round.' I agreed with him, of course!

The two biggest crowd pullers in British boxing in the sixties were Henry Cooper and West Ham 'Golden boy' Billy Walker. There was not a spare seat to be had when Henry defended his British heavyweight championship against battling Billy at Wembley in 1967. The predictions were that Walker's best chance of winning was on a cut eye. Ironically, that was how he lost. The referee stopped it in the sixth round to give Our Enery a record third Lonsdale Belt outright.

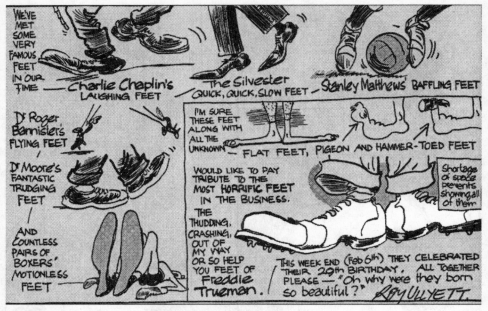

I finish my journey back into the swinging sixties with the biggest swinger of them all, fiery Fred Trueman. I wished his famous feet a happy twenty ninth birthday (above), and put him forward as a possible catwalk candidate (left) when there was a story about a shortage of fashion models. Fred and I went to Buckingham Palace on the same day in 1989 to collect our OBEs. He deserved a knighthood for his services to cartoonists in general and to me in particular. Thank you, Fred, for using up so much of my lead.

This is something of an historic cartoon in as much as it is the first ever signed by Prince Philip. It was drawn to mark his installation in 1960 as a Companion Rat of the Grand Order of Water Rats. The signed original became the property of the GOWR, my favourite charity organisation.

6: A Rat, and Proud of It!

I HAVE been a Rat for half my life, and very proud of it. It was back in 1955 when my distinguished *Daily Express* colleague Percy (later Sir Percy) Hoskins, the greatest of all crime reporters, asked me to design a menu for the Grand Order of Water Rats. This is the charity organisation set up back in 1889, and to which caring members of the show business and entertainment world give their time, their money and their energy to help those less fortunate than themselves. I was warmly welcomed to the Rats by future King Rat Johnnie Riscoe.

Cockney comedian Tommy Trinder was the first King Rat featured on the front cover of the brochure, and every year since I have had the honour of drawing the new King Rat and presenting him with the framed original at his inauguration. I perform the same service for the lovely Lady Ratlings, and also for the Variety Club Golfing Society.

The Rats kindly made me one of only twenty Companion Rats, and among my illustrious fellow Companions are Prince Philip and the Prince of Wales. I auctioned one of my cartoons of the Duke of Edinburgh at a Grand Water Rats dinner, where Paul Raymond – he of girlie world fame – made the top charity-boosting bid of £2,500. I said that it was the first picture he had ever possessed of somebody fully clothed!

Prince Philip and Prince Charles share a great sense of humour, as they proved when we were together at the top table at a GOWR lunch. During my speech I made reference to the fact that Prince Charles had been beaten that week in a horse race. I asked what went wrong, and Prince Philip jumped in with the comment, 'He was too bloody slow!' Another time at a cricket dinner for Sir Don Bradman, Prince Charles led the laughter when I said that whenever His Royal Highness went into bat he always wore two boxes to protect the dynasty.

I am flattered to have my cartoons decorating the GOWR headquarters. They also hung proudly in the old and much-missed Press Club, and mine was among the first to be displayed in The Cartoonist pub just off Fleet Street. Here followeth just a sample of my cartooning work away from the world of sport.

This portrayal of my dear old pal Bud Flanagan was auctioned for £5,550, and the money helped boost the Leukaemia Fund that he set up in memory of his son. The painting was blown up to life size, and fund supporters had their photographs taken with it in return for a donation. Sadly, Bud himself died of Leukaemia in 1968. There will never be another like him. His name, and the Fund, live on at Royal Marsden Hospital.

Paul Daniels said that he liked this front cover that I designed (but not a lot) for his year as King Rat. It marked the fortieth anniversary since my first Water Rats tribute to comedian Tommy Trinder.

I was proud and privileged to be asked to draw this brochure front cover for the reunion of Muhammad Ali and Henry Cooper. Two super sportsmen, two super people.

Prince Philip was celebrating his twenty-fifth year as a Companion Rat when I drew this. Davy Kaye, the King Rat, just about came up to the Prince's naval navel.

The Water Rats have supported the Duke of Edinburgh's Award Scheme since its inception, and I drew this for a dinner in aid of the project. Ho-de-ho!

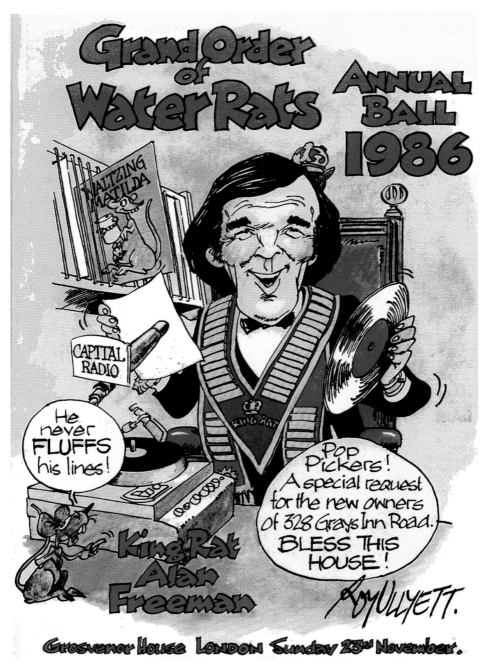

Alan 'Fluff' Freeman was King Rat in 1986, and welcomed the opening of the GOWR's new headquarters at Gray's Inn Road in the heart of London.

Harry Secombe was an enthusiastic golfer. When a gale came up during one of the Variety Club tournaments, he announced that he was doing a re-make of Goon with the Wind. This cartoon marked his year as Variety Golf Society captain.

Eddie Large might have been a professional footballer, but for being knocked down by a bus when he was a lad on Manchester City's books. Golf became his new passion, and he was a popular captain of the Variety Club Golfing Society.

Les Dawson was one of my favourite comedians. He told me when I presented him with the framed original of this drawing, 'I can take it to the bank to prove that I am not overdrawn!' King Rat Les was a very funny man.

It was a swing-along-a-Max year when Max Bygraves became captain of the Variety Club Golfing Society, which has as its aim the raising of money for Sunshine Coaches for underprivileged children while encouraging the pursuit and pleasure of golf.

116

Roy Hudd, a walking, talking record book on my favourite subject of the music-hall, was a fitting King Rat in the Centenary Year of the GOWR.

117

Tarby looks nothing like this now, of course, but this was when he had a head of hair you could nest in. Jimmy is an exceptional golfer, and could have made it as a professional if he had not been so busy making people laugh.

118

Ronnie Corbett was kind enough to say that this was one of his favourite cartoons of himself. He might be a little man, but Ronnie is a giant of showbusiness.

When Trevor Brooking first saw this, he could not help pointing out that he headed the winning goal for West Ham in the 1980 FA Cup final. Yes, Trevor, for once the glory went to your head!

Russ Abbot insists that his Flying Officer Kite character was NOT based on Flying Officer R.H.F. Ullyett! The matter is in the hands of my solicitors, Sue, Grabbit and Run.

Bob Hope asked me to convey this message before the 'Bob Hope British Classic' at the RAC Country Club at Epsom in 1980. Hope sprung eternal on the golf course.

7: Walking on Water

CLOWNING WITH CLOUGHIE, IN THE LAIR OF THE GOLDEN BEAR, SAYING GOODBYE TO GREAVSIE, HELLO TO LILLEE AND THOMSON, AU REVOIR TO SIR ALF AND FAREWELL TO GILES

THE seventies were about players with perms, high-heeled shoes, kipper ties and flares ... but there was not a lot of flair on the playing fields of England. It was an angry decade, with trouble on the terraces, violence on the football pitch and the poison of politics in the cricket world. The hardest thing to find as the suddenly commercialised sports scene lost its innocence was *humour*. Thank goodness, then, for Cloughie!

Brian Clough continually came to the rescue of this cartoonist trying to bring a smile to the country's breakfast tables. Whether managing at Derby County, Leeds United, Brighton or Nottingham Forest, or addressing the nation on television, he was like a walking, talking caricature just crying out for recognition from my pen.

I often wonder how I would have carried out my job as a sports cartoonist without two wonderfully and at times outrageously outspoken Yorkshiremen to fuel my imagination and fill my sketch pad. Cloughie took over from Fred Trueman as my greatest pen pal. He was the first football manager to really get to the grips with the growing

phenomenon of television's power in sport. He turned the TV set into his soapbox, and one night surpassed himself by going to the extremes of describing Poland's goalkeeper as a clown. It was during a match in which the goalie made a series of quite miraculous saves to eliminate England from the World Cup and virtually bring an end to the international career of another great favourite of mine, Sir Alf Ramsey. Through this cartoonist's eyes it was Cloughie who was more the clown.

He was so prolific and po-faced with his pontifications that I started to portray him as thinking he could walk to work on the Trent. Good old Cloughie responded by sending a message to me through the ebullient Midlands football correspondent for the *Express*, Alan Williams: 'Young man, kindly inform that cartoon chappie Roy Ullyet that I do not think I can walk on water. I *know* I bloody can!'

Cloughie went right up in my estimation. It proved that he could laugh at himself. One thing I have learned during my eight decades on this puzzling and at times perplexing planet is that you must never take yourself or the world too seriously. That way lies madness. A cartoonist's motto has to be, 'laugh and the world laughs with you'.

Mind you, even I struggled to find the funny side of odd goings on at the *Express*. An enthusiastic chap with a distinctive Berkshire burr, Ken Lawrence, took over from John Morgan as sports editor in 1972. I realised he had a good sense of humour when one of the first things he tried to do was pick a fight with the *Daily Express* racing twins, Peter O'Sullevan and Clive 'The Scout' Graham. They were without any doubt the two best read and most authoritative racing correspondents in the business. You could almost hear the sharp intake of breath around the office when it was revealed that Lawrence was about to fire O'Sullevan. It was something akin to the Indians scalping John Wayne. This,

The pressure started to mount on poor old Alf Ramsey when England failed to qualify for the 1974 World Cup. He was finally kicked out by the Football Association with what I thought was less than good grace considering all that he had achieved for the English game. He may not have done it with a smile, but he was nearly always dignified, and had the total respect and loyalty of his players. The same, I am afraid, could not be said of his successor Don Revie, who was irreverently known to my football writing colleagues as, 'Don Readies'. The Don was a brilliant club manager, but never seemed suited to the England job that he deserted to join the Arabs.

126

following fast on the heels of a daft decision to force Desmond Hackett out of the paper, made no sense whatsoever to me. But what do I know? I am just a simple sports cartoonist with my brains in my pencil.

The gentle and unflappable O'Sullevan, now Sir Peter, who recently hung up his microphone as the unmistakable Voice of Racing, famously dubbed Ken as Lawrence of Siberia. He had powerful friends 'upstairs' where the *Express* was still being run by the remnants of the Beaverbrook empire. A quiet word in a couple of ears, and Peter and Clive Graham were awarded new contracts at what was rumoured to be double their money.

Undaunted, Ken Lawrence survived this shaky start and from then on ran the sports department with a kindly manner that made nonsense of his initial Atilla the Hun approach. He proved he knew the value of a good laugh on the sports pages by hiring Eric Morecambe to contribute a weekly column which I illustrated.

Eric's first column coincided with the appointment of Don Revie as England manager after my old pen friend Sir Alf Ramsey had been Pole-axed following England's exit from the 1974 World Cup campaign. Asked what he would do if he were in Revie's shoes, Eric told *Express* readers: 'I would walk with a limp. They are a size too small.'

In a later column, Eric tackled the issue of whether goals should be made bigger because of the dominance of defences. 'No, sunshine,' he said, 'the answer to the problem is not bigger goals but smaller goalkeepers.' Priceless stuff.

There were mutterings about Eric taking money from the *Express* that he hardly needed at a time when his scintillating double act with Ernie Wise was the top comedy draw in the country. But I know for a fact that Eric used to have his fee paid directly to Luton Town Football Club, where he was an enthusiastic director.

I just about remember an extremely liquid lunch at the Cheshire Cheese in Fleet Street where Eric and I were guests of the new and very momentary *Express* editor, Sir Alastair Burnet. Even by Fleet Street standards, it was a heavy drinking session and when it came time for Eric to be picked up by his chauffeur he was struggling to walk on legs that were suddenly betraying him. We held him up against the wall of the *Daily Telegraph* office building while waiting for his car to arrive, and quickly gathered a crowd as by-passers spotted Eric and thought that he was putting on an act for them. As we poured him into his car, the comedian came to the surface and he shouted, 'I'm not as think as you drunk I am!' What a lovely and very funny man he was. They don't make them like him any more.

Tempus was fugiting, and in the New Year of 1974 my colleagues surprised me in the nicest possible way. They staged a special presentation at our favourite Fleet Street watering hole El Vino's to mark my twenty-one years as an *Express* cartoonist. I wonder what dear Arthur Christiansen Up There in the great editorial department in the sky thought when he saw his Four Cartooning Musketeers gathered together for the evening: Osbert Lancaster, Michael Cummings, Carl Giles and myself. Also drawn into the ceremony were Barry Appleby, who I had pipped to the *Star* job all those years ago, and JAK, the cartooning master from our then sister paper, the *Evening Standard*. I am not sure if there is a collective noun for a gathering of cartoonists, but let me invent one by saying it was a chuckle of cartoonists. We had a lot to laugh about because Ted Heath had just introduced the three-day working week in his battle with the striking coalminers. Osbert said in that lovely dry way of his, 'I'm not going to work an extra day for any bugger.'

Sir Trevor Evans and Sir Percy Hoskins, two distinguished *Express* journalists, made flattering speeches about what a jolly good chap I was (hear, hear), and I was presented with a magnificent Giles cartoon showing me as a sporting all-rounder, plus a silver tankard inscribed, ROY ULLYETT: GOOD COMPANION OF FLEET STREET, NEW YEAR 1974. Who would have thought that it would be another twenty-one years before I hung up my pen? Old cartoonists never die. They just run out of lead.

Carl Giles was, of course, an institution. I treasure his cartoon of me, which adorns a wall at my home. Genius is a word bandied around too readily, but it certainly sat comfortably on Carl's sturdy shoulders. He was born two years after me (1916) in the Arsenal territory of Islington, but it was his adopted county of Suffolk with which he became most closely associated. There, in a penthouse studio overlooking the Buttermarket in Ipswich, he used to create his masterpieces

Giles had Grandma handbagging me in a note complaining about my treatment of his Ipswich Town team.

featuring his much-loved 'Crisis Family', with the permanently harassed father, irate mother, currant-eyed, mischievous children, the hypochondriac Vera, and the skull-headed headmaster Chalkie. And who will ever forget his greatest creation, Grandma, who was left over from the Victorian age with the bird in her hat, umbrella in hand, fox fur round her neck and, according to Carl, 'reeking of bombazine' (a twilled fabric, usually of worsted and worn dyed

The one and only Carl Giles painted this cartoon of me, and is a treasured possession despite the fact that he added at least two stone to my bulk.

I take a one-eyed view of Tony Jacklin and the famous claret jug Open trophy

black by mourning Victorian widows). Giles said that he modelled Grandma on one of his own grandmothers, whom, he said, never quite adjusted to the 20th Century. The truth is that Carl used to put his OWN face on to Grandma!

Like me, Giles never had a drawing lesson in his life. His mastery of perspective came naturally, and was perfected over the years by all-important observation. He built a caravan studio in the 1950s, and used to travel around the country sketching anything that took his eye. I say 'eye' quite deliberately because it is a little-known fact that Britain's most popular cartoonist had sight in only one eye. He became partially sighted following a pre-war motorcycle accident when he was just starting out on his career as a cartoon animator. As you can see from the drawing above, having sight in only one eye need not be too big a handicap for a cartoonist. When I am zooming in on a subject, I often close my right eye. Giles certainly showed no signs of his handicap. He was an expert animator, and he retained his close interest in film cartoons throughout his life, although it was for his newspaper work that he was known and loved throughout the land.

I was extremely fond of Carl, and a great admirer of his work, but I have to say you never quite knew how he would be from one meeting to the next. He was a curious mixture of geniality and grumpiness, and there were, I know, several times when *Express* editors had to bend over backwards to talk him out of resigning. Most times, though, he was in an amiable mood. He could be gregarious and fond of a drink or three and he was a serious smoker.

Sadly, Carl did not have an easy passage into old age. He had both legs amputated, and was confined to a wheelchair by the time the good folk of Ipswich honoured him by erecting a statue depicting the unforgettable Grandma Giles, the snivelling Vera and Butch, the loveable family dog. You could feel the warmth generated by Carl and his cartoons at his memorial service at St Bride's in Fleet Street in 1995 following his passing at the age of 78.

I was proud to decorate the same *Express* newspapers as Carl for most of the five decades that he was flourishing his works of art. His genius lay in the way he drew not only his characters but also their surroundings and the elements. His rain made you feel wet. You sensed you could make a snowball out of his snow. You could warm your hands on the fires in the hearth, and he could freeze you to the bone with winter storms that turned Grandma's umbrella inside out and parted her from her beloved hat.

The lesson would-be cartoonists can learn from Giles is never be frightened of white space. Carl was a master at using acres of white space to accentuate his subject. The golden rule is, *what you leave out can be as important as what you put in*.

Yes, I treasure my Carl Giles cartoon, and the memory of having a final bottle of bubbly with him before he passed on. Cheers, Carl.

Much of the seventies seemed about the retirements of my favourite sports people. Des Hackett, Fred Trueman, Colin Milburn, Henry Cooper, Matt Busby, Alf Ramsey, George Best, Denis Law, Bobby and Jack Charlton and Jimmy Greaves all bowed out. It was as if they were all conspiring to put this cartoonist out of work! Greavsie was the finest finisher I ever saw, and I marked his exit from the soccer stage with a cartoon in which I underlined that his phenomenal goal scoring record was the sort of total football we all understood. Jimmy asked for the original, and just recently was kind enough to say, 'It hangs on the wall at my daughter's home, and is a treasured possession. When my grandchildren ask me what I used to do, I point to the cartoon. It sums up better than a book what my football career was about.' Bless you, James, and thank you for all the pleasure you gave me with your goals, from your spikey-haired days as a fleet-footed

131

artful dodger at Chelsea to those defence-denting performances with Tottenham and England. You have plenty to tell your grandchildren.

On the cricket front, two more Yorkshiremen – Ray Illingworth and Geoff Boycott – kept me going following the departure of the one and only fiery Fred. A magnificent new fast bowler took my eye. Unfortunately he was Australian. Dennis Lillee bowled with all the ferocity and fire of Trueman, and England's batsmen quivered and collapsed under the twin assaults of Lillee and Thomson (or Lilian Thomson, as Eric Morecambe always referred to them).

Lillee was a fierce competitor, but he always found time for some banter with his favourite umpire, Dickie Bird. Once, after Dickie had turned down his loud LBW appeal, Dennis said: 'I think that your eyesight is going, Dickie.'

'No,' said Dickie, 'it's *your* eyesight that's going. I'm the ice cream seller.'

John Snow was another fast bowler with a good sense of humour. The Sussex and England player came roaring in to bowl to the Leicestershire batsman Paul Marner, who went on to his back foot to hook what was a loose full toss. As his bat connected, the 'ball'

Dennis Lillee on the rampage

disintegrated. Snow and the rest of the Sussex team were on their knees in helpless laughter. He had bowled a round bar of red soap. John said that he was trying to clean bowl Marner. Now that's the sort fun we need in a sports world that is too often about snarling and not enough about smiling.

While so many of my favourite sportsmen were bowing out, I was sad that one of my friends was stubbornly refusing to leave the stage. Muhammad Ali insisted on fighting on after a series of hard battles, and I delivered a warning in cartoon form about the dangers of going downhill. Sadly, the great man refused to listen and his health deteriorated rapidly after he had taken a dreadful beating from Larry Holmes in a fight too far. At his peak, Ali would have boxed Larry's ears off. Ali's three wars with Joe Frazier during the seventies took an enormous toll, and his astonishing victory over George Foreman in the Rumble in the

132

The first Ali-Frazier fight in New York in 1971 lived up to its billing as the Fight of the Century. Ali was floored by a terrific left hook in the fifteenth and final round, and this swayed a close points decision in Frazier's favour. Ali won the second North American title fight on points over twelve rounds in 1974, and then in 1975 they knocked each other to the edge of exhaustion in their 'Thrilla in Manila' which Ali won when Smokin' Joe retired at the end of fourteen viciously hard rounds. I thought that Ali should have retired there and then, and my cartoon on the right was a warning of the dangers of going downhill in boxing.

Jungle in Zaire was achieved at what cost to his health? You cannot tell me that laying on the ropes allowing Foreman to punch himself out helped his physical condition in later life. Ali was the Great Entertainer, and like so many great entertainers he just did not know when to leave the stage. But I thank him from the bottom of my pencil for the drawing pleasure that he gave me over a span of more than twenty years.

Golf carried on enjoying a boom in the seventies. Jack Nicklaus, the Golden

Bear, took over where Arnie Palmer had left off and he dominated the world's greens. What I admired most about Jack, apart from his mastery of golf, was his victory in the battle of the bulge. In his early visits to our shores I always depicted him as the Fat Man of the fairways (see facing page), but he got his weight under control and cleaned up more majors than any other golfer in history. Tom Watson gave him a run for his money, and their head-to-head duel in the 1977 Open at Turnberry was golf at its greatest. This deserved an oil painting rather than a cartoon.

Jack was another real gentleman of golf, and I had some enjoyable social evenings with him and his wife when he was winding down during high-pressure tournaments. I first saw Jack play as an amateur in 1957, and throughout all the years that I have known him he has always represented his sport with a dignity and grace that should serve as an example to all. What I admire about him is that he has somehow managed to retain an approach to the game that is, in spirit at least, basically that of his amateur days. He has always accepted defeat and triumph alike and, in the words of Rudyard Kipling, 'has treated those two imposters just the same'.

I hope you do not consider this the ramblings of a daft old man, but I have been around the world's golf circuit for long enough to be able to make the statement

that professional golfers are a credit to professional sport. I just wish some of the spoilt-brat footballers I have come across – with their obscenely fat wage packets, flash cars and appalling manners – could take a lesson in how to conduct themselves from the likes of gentlemen like Jack Nicklaus, Henry Cotton, Peter Thomson, Johnny Miller, Tom Watson, Arnold Palmer, Gary Player ... I could go on and on. An over-the-top view? Well I don't think so.

I cannot put Lee Trevino in the 'great gentlemen of golf' category, but I put him near the top as an entertainer. While he could be irritating to some of his opponents with his non-stop chatter, Lee always gave the galleries something worthwhile to watch and jaw about ... and cartoonists like me something to draw about. He reminded me in some ways of a lovely Irish golfer called Fred Daly, who won the British Open in 1947. I used to walk around the course with

Fred, and he always had time for a chat as he strolled between each shot. Nothing seemed to phase him and, like Trevino, he could charm the birds down out of the trees and then teach them to sing. Fred often used to whistle while he worked, thoroughly enjoying himself as he sauntered around the course as if on a Sunday afternoon stroll. Max Faulkner, who used to dress as colourfully as Max Miller, was the cheeky chappie of the fairways, and was another who could be enjoyable company on and off the course. Max, Open champion at Portrush in 1951, was a flamboyant character, who was always tinkering with his clubs. He used to disappear into his workshop and come out with a new club that he had just made himself. One amazing putter that he used with success for several years consisted of a billiard cue for a shaft and a wooden head that Max had sculpted from a piece of driftwood that he had found while walking along a beach. He could be confident to the point of cockiness, and with one round still to go in the 1951 Open was signing his autograph, 'Max Faulkner, Open Champion 1951'. Of course, he provided action to go with the words. What a character.

Trevino has the same sort of winning personality, and lights up the course with his presence. He has a non-stop supply of golfing anecdotes, most of which are made up but which he spins to give them a touch of believability. On his way to winning the first of his two back-to-back British Opens at Royal Birkdale in 1971, he said, 'I realised the caddie I had in my last tournament in the States was a novice after I had driven off from the first tee. I asked him how far I was from the green. "About three blocks," came the reply.'

It was this 1971 championship in which Trevino beat Lu Liang Huan by one shot. Dubbed Mr Lu by master TV commentator Peter Alliss (who drew my attention throughout his own smooth-swinging career), the man from Formosa captured the public imagination with his impeccable manners and smooth golf.

During one of his rounds, Mr Lu hooked a shot into the gallery. His ball hit a woman spectator and she was taken to hospital for treatment. At the end of his round, Mr Lu visited the woman and presented her with a box of half a dozen golf balls. 'Now,' he said, 'you throw at me.'

All these professional golfers could reach prodigious distances off the tee, but I do not think many of them have bettered my longest ever drive of 410 metres. I achieved this in a competition in Majorca in 1977 to find the biggest hitter. I finished only third, and the winner got close to 500 metres.

I suppose I should tell you that the competition was not staged on a golf course but at an airport! A team of golfing journalists were invited to take part to mark the opening of a new runway at Palma airport. The ball just ran and ran. It gave a whole new meaning to an air shot.

With the encouragement of the three wise men of the sports department – Ken Lawrence, his jolly deputy Norman Dixon and chief sub-editor Don Woodward – I developed my own dead-beat football team that I had first introduced to *Express* readers back in the 1950s. In transfer market terms they were worth, uh, nothing. The unquestioned hero of the team was a bespectacled, butter-fingered, brainless goalkeeper who became such a star that he used to get fan mail. Bobby Charlton dropped me a line to say, 'Here at United we consider your goalkeeper worthy of the Footballer of the Year award.' Arsenal coach Don Howe said that he could identify the players on which I had based my drawings. I now dedicate the next two pages to old Goalfingers before moving on to proper celebrities who helped colour the seventies.

From the ridiculous to the sublime. My fumbling Goalfingers character was the antithesis to Gordon Banks, who was quite comfortably the greatest goalkeeper I ever had the pleasure of drawing. Peter Shilton, Pat Jennings, Frank Swift and David Seaman ran him close, but he was a fingertip ahead of them all. What a tragedy in 1972 when a car smash cost him the sight of an eye and his career. I reckon Gordon had at least another eight years of top-flight football left in him. He was as safe as the Banks of England.

Gordon — WORLD'S GREATEST.

Leeds United were heavily criticised for the ruthless streak in their football in the early seventies, but manager Don Revie and his skipper Billy Bremner worked hard at improving their image (below right). They won the Centenary FA Cup final against Arsenal (above) after losing out on a treble in another eventful season (below left).

141

The one and only Lester Piggott was on the receiving end of my pencil for more than forty years. I followed him from when he first burst on to the scene as a chubby faced schoolboy jockey in 1948 through to his record setting 30th Classic victory. I often met Lester in the company of his close friend Peter O'Sullevan. He was always hidden behind a huge cigar, and to be honest I hardly ever understood a word he said to me. But what a jockey! I also met Red Rum at Aintree, and I did not understand what he said to me either!

I did a little sticking up for the Royals ... first of all sticking my fingers up to Harvey Smith on behalf of Prince Anne after he had said that she should not be considered for the equestrian team for the Olympics. Anne was a brilliant horsewoman and deserved to get into the British team on merit. I also did my little bit to ridicule the miserable Annigoni portrait of the Queen that caused so much controversy. I have had the pleasure of meeting Her Majesty on several occasions, and can state quite categorically that the portrait did not do her justice. She radiates warmth with a smile that could warm the cockles of an Eskimo. Her Majesty would have been better off being cartooned! Bad portraits can do more damage than any tell-tale book or vitriolic article. Paintings, even some cartoons, tend to hang around for ever.

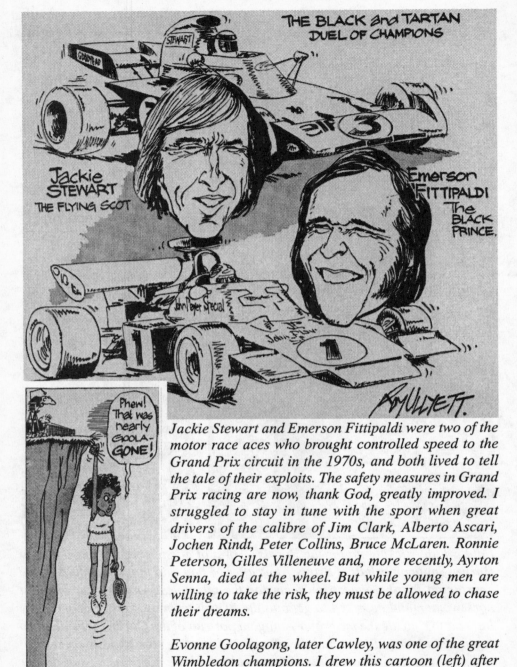

THE BLACK and TARTAN
DUEL OF CHAMPIONS

Jackie
STEWART
THE FLYING SCOT

Emerson
FITTIPALDI
The
BLACK
PRINCE.

Phew!
That was
nearly
GOOLA-
GONE!

Jackie Stewart and Emerson Fittipaldi were two of the motor race aces who brought controlled speed to the Grand Prix circuit in the 1970s, and both lived to tell the tale of their exploits. The safety measures in Grand Prix racing are now, thank God, greatly improved. I struggled to stay in tune with the sport when great drivers of the calibre of Jim Clark, Alberto Ascari, Jochen Rindt, Peter Collins, Bruce McLaren. Ronnie Peterson, Gilles Villeneuve and, more recently, Ayrton Senna, died at the wheel. But while young men are willing to take the risk, they must be allowed to chase their dreams.

Evonne Goolagong, later Cawley, was one of the great Wimbledon champions. I drew this cartoon (left) after she had survived a tough semi-final. She was so lithe and graceful, and rivalled Billie-Jean King, Chris Evert, Margaret Smith (Court), Maria Bueno, Martina Navratilova and Steffi Graf as the queen of the courts.

144

Where would I have been without Yorkshiremen to keep me in work? Ray Illingworth (above left) and Geoff Boycott took over from Fred Trueman as favourite targets for my pencil. Both gave me plenty of ammunition with their actions on the pitch and their words off it.

A big light went out in my cartooning world with the retirement of Olly Milburn, who made a huge impact during a cricketing career tragically cut short when he lost the sight of an eye in a car smash. He asked me for the original of the drawing on the left, and I was only too pleased to let him have it. He deserved a send-off in oils.

145

Nobby Stiles hung up his boots in 1974, and to mark his passing out parade I repeated a drawing of him at the greatest moment in his life. Nobody who saw it will ever forget his joyful celebration of England's victory in the 1966 World Cup final. He hopped around the Wembley pitch like a drunken goblin. Nobby was a hard little man, but he was usually fair and always gave 110 per cent when wearing the England and Manchester United shirts.

THANKS FOR THE MEMORIES NOBBY. NOW YOU CAN PUT YOUR TEETH BACK IN AND YOUR FEET UP. YOU DID US PROUD.

More memories of 1966 and all that. I drew Bobby Moore holding aloft the Jules Rimet trophy as England prepared to defend the championship in Mexico in 1970. The week this appeared in the Express, Bobby was arrested in Bogota on a trumped-up jewel theft charge. All those of us who knew Bobby well realised that he would not take a liberty, let alone steal a bracelet. He was, of course, released by the Colombian police who could not make the charge stick. He then proceeded to prove during the tournament that he was, as Pele said, the best defender in the world.

Two years after England's defeat by West Germany in the 1970 World Cup quarter-final the two teams met again, this time in a European championship match at Wembley. Brian Clough controversially withdrew Roy McFarland at the last minute, and England played without a recognised centre-half. This was suicidal against a side boasting the goal power of 'Der Bomber' Gerd Muller, and he scored one of the goals in a 3-1 German victory. I thought my cartoon on the left captured the depressed feelings of the nation.

David Bedford (left) and Tommy Docherty (below) were two great characters who helped me pencil my way through the 1970s. Bedford brought much-needed attention to the track with his bold style of front running. He played a major part in re-establishing the popularity of athletics in Britain in the seventies after a drop in public interest. His extrovert appearance, including a drooping Mexican moustache and red socks, delighted the crowds. He disappointed in the major championships when he paid the price of not having a finishing kick, but against the clock Britain has had few more successful middle-distance runners.

Tommy Docherty was always good for a laugh during a see-saw managerial career when, to quote him, he had more clubs than Jack Nicklaus. This cartoon was drawn when he was in charge at Manchester United and under fire for their robust play. When Tommy saw it in the Express *he challenged me to a duel –* handbags at ten paces!

There were no more exciting British fighters in the seventies than John Conteh and Chris Finnegan. They carried on the great ring traditions set by Randolph Turpin and Freddie Mills. Conteh beat Finnegan in their two meetings and went on to win the world light-heavyweight crown before getting tied up in out-of-the-ring boxing politics that affected his boxing form. Big-hearted Finnegan challenged Bob Foster for the world light-heavyweight crown, but it was a bridge too far and he went down and out to Foster's fearsome left hook in the fourteenth round.

150

I considered Harry Gibbs one of our better referees, but I am convinced that he called it wrong when he decided Joe Bugner had beaten Henry Cooper on points in their triple title fight at Wembley in 1971. Bugner, a baby of 21 compared to the 36-year-old Cooper, just did not do enough for my money to take the titles from Henry, who was uncharacteristically bitter and angry in defeat. He usually carried himself with great dignity, but on this occasion he just could not hide his disappointment. The majority in the crowd agreed with his view that he had won what was to prove his final fight.

151

This was my farewell message to Our 'Enery when he announced his retirement from the ring in 1971. There has never been a more popular British ring hero.

I enjoyed having fun at the expense of my good friend Tony Jacklin. He ignored my expert advice on moustache maintenance, and was soon back to being clean shaven. I was surprised he wanted extra weight on his lip when he was so concerned about the pounds he was putting on (right). Jacko was wined and dined to such an extent after his US and British Open victories that he was busting out all over. What a gift he was for a cartoonist!

153

After more than forty years on the fairways (and often in the rough) I felt I was well qualified to give readers a lesson in how not to drive off from the tee. My old partners at Thorpe Hall Golf Club, Thorpe Bay, will recognise the swing.

8: Farewell Fleet Street

THE END OF THE BEAVERBROOK
EMPIRE, AND THE CLOSING DOWN
OF FLEET STREET, BUT I HAVE
SUPERBRAT McENROE, BOYCS AND
BOTHAM TO KEEP ME IN BUSINESS.

WHATEVER happened to Fleet Street? The newspaper village – for that is what it was – suddenly disappeared, as dear old Arthur Askey used to say, 'before your very eyes'. In what seemed no more time for it to take the sun to set, the world's largest concentrated publishing empire vanished as newspapers moved headquarters to different parts of London to make way for City types more interested in stocks and shares than deadlines and headlines. Did the Street of Ink die? No, it just evaporated away, leaving an old sports cartoonist very sad and confused.

The bars – El Vino's, the Albion, Poppins, Mucky Duck, King and Keys, Cheshire Cheese *et al* – remained crowded, but the talk was now of insurance policies and index-linked portfolios rather than royal scandals and hot gossip from the worlds of sport and politics. Where ink-stained printers had stood shoulder to shoulder, jar to jar, jaw to jaw with journalists loudly discussing breaking news stories and edition times, there were tiny gentlemen from the east yacking about the yen and well-heeled bankers and businessmen plotting the next takeover. Wickedly, I knew where I wanted to stick my pencil.

They had put padlocks on the doors of the ugly or beautiful (according to your architectural taste) black-glass *Express* building where I had spent the best years of my life. The Black Lubianka, *Private Eye* called it. This is where I had met thousands of deadlines, drawn an army of faces, raised (I hope) a few laughs, and seen a procession of editors come and go in the bid to stop the circulation drain that started following the 1958 departure of the great Arthur Christiansen. Among those I can remember following in his footsteps were Sir Edward Pickering, Bob Edwards, Derek Marks, Ian McColl, Sir Alastair Burnet, Roy Wright, Derek Jameson, Arthur Firth, Christopher Ward, Nick Lloyd and, the man in charge when I finally departed, Richard Addis. I saw off more editors than Robber Maxwell had hot bagels. Now they had put a padlock on the door.

They could shut down the building, but not my memories. The Black Lubianka had been my cruise ship on a voyage of more fun and adventure than any one

A cartoon featuring one of my editors after he had returned to reading the news

"WITH FOOTBALL BLACKED OUT, SIR ALASTAIR, WEST HAM UNITED'S SPONSORS WERE WONDERING WHETHER YOU'D WEAR THIS SHIRT WHEN YOU READ THE NEWS?"

man should be allowed. Even now I can see clearly the grand art deco entrance lobby, and the extravagant sweep of stairs winding on a majestic course past a first landing from which stared the sculpted head of Lord Beaverbrook, looking fit to haunt the place. The decor was all yellowish marble and chrome light fittings like the most garish of 1930s picture palaces. This way for the three and nines. The interior designers had pulled off a triple whammy. It was opulent, ornate and obscene, all at the same time.

Either side of the foot of the stairs was a small, thick-carpeted lift, operated by cheerful uniformed Beaverbrook disciples who had been given work despite (or because of) disabilities, many of them old war veterans. The Beaver and his former flying ace son, Max Aitken, loved and respected anybody who had done his bit in the war.

Most prominent of all in the lobby above an American hotel-style reception desk was the huge Crusader with his shield and sword ready for battle. You were left in no doubt that this was a crusading newspaper. Lord Beaverbrook loved to get his teeth into the big political issues of the day, and he would use his organ to run personal vendettas ('Now there's a novelty,' I can hear Eric Morecambe saying). The Beaver was less than amused when I once told him, only half jokingly, 'Anyone starting at page one of the paper and reading all the way through deserves a laugh if they get to the back.'

I got on famously with Sir Max Aitken, the Beaver's son who inherited the empire and, unfortunately, supervised its gradual decline and fall. As an ex-RAF man who had been decorated with the DFC and DSO, he loved my moustache and said that it made him feel nostalgic for the days when he was a crack fighter pilot. I achieved no heroics, but just the fact that I had served in the RAF gave us an unbreakable bond. He was always keen to chat about his yachting, power boating and Arsenal Football Club, and only seemed out of his depth when it came to matters of the newspaper. Max had at last been given the train set, but did not really know how to run it compared with his self-made dad, who was a born entrepreneur. He brought in the energetic, and at times eccentric, Jocelyn Stevens to put a finger in the dam in the mid-1960s, but the paper was sinking fast. Trafalgar House, under the stewardship of Victor (later Lord) Matthews, took over in the early 1980s, but it was a company with no real heart and feeling for newspapers. There was no black ink in their blood.

Then it was the turn of United Newspapers to take control, with Lord Stephens running the show. Next up, yet another Lord – this time Lord Hollick, who was as far removed from old Lord Beaverbrook as the Spice Girls to Enrico Caruso. The *Express* moved across Blackfriars Bridge to a smart new building overlooking the Thames. But my heart stayed a mile and a smile away in Fleet Street. For more than fifty years, the Street had been my second home. I would commute there nearly every day from my home in Westcliff-on-Sea in Essex, taking the 'Misery Line' train to Fenchurch Street. We poor, put-upon passengers did our best to laugh our way to work despite the pitiful efforts of British Rail trying (and failing) to run their trains on time. And now here I am into galloping old age feeling nostalgic for those frustrating days when the Southend-to-Fenchurch-Street line was about as reliable as an Italian tank.

I had shared my office for forty-odd years with Michael Cummings, the pungent political cartoonist who gave the old *Express* leader pages a distinctive look with his meticulously created drawings. Suddenly they changed the format of the paper from broadsheet to a tabloid, and Michael and I felt as if we had been shunted from a ballroom to a rabbit hutch. New format, new location, new technology. Things would never be the same again.

When I officially retired in 1979 after my sixty-fifth birthday Cummings penned one of his carefully crafted cartoons that was presented to me at my leaving lunch. Even more memorable than the lunch was the fact that I was privileged to be 'drummed out'. It was a decades-old Fleet Street tradition usually exclusive to printers. When any of them retired they would go the stone – where the pages of type were pieced together by compositors – and walk out for the last time while colleagues hammered the stone with their tools and type galleys.

The cartoon that Cummings drew for my retirement lunch in 1979.

They kindly and movingly treated me to one of these emotional send offs, little knowing that before long they would all be unceremoniously dumped rather than drummed out following the switch to new technology. How tragic.

My retirement was one of the shortest on record. I was back in the paper the following Monday and continued to submit regular cartoons in a freelance capacity – still going to the office – until I was dragged kicking and screaming into retirement in May 1997 as the *Express* entered a new era as a seven-day paper. I had the best 44 years of my life, so far, with the paper, and I wish my old colleagues the best of luck as they move boldly towards the new millenium with their new style paper under the intelligent direction of my last editor, Richard Addis.

The last thing I want to do is depress anybody with my memories, but I *know* that my days were the best days. The switch to computers, faxes, scanners, mobiles and modems has made news-gathering and publishing swifter, cost effective and more efficient, but fast food will never taste better than that which is slowly and lovingly cooked. This old man thinks that the soul has gone out of the business. The special camaraderie that existed in the 'village' of Fleet Street has, I am sad to say, disappeared for ever.

I go back there now only for the occasional memorial service at St Bride's Church. In recent years I have made sad journeys to say farewell to Carl Giles, my old sports editor John Morgan and the columnist who always entertained, Desmond Hackett. It was a great privilege to illustrate the front covers of the memorial service programmes for both John and Des, who were good buddies of mine as well as colleagues. Donald Saunders, former distinguished *Daily*

I said farewell in 1992 to two of my old Express colleagues, John Morgan (above left) and Des Hackett, who always addressed everybody as 'my old commander' because he had a terrible memory for names. These drawings were used to illustrate their memorial service programmes at St Bride's Church in Fleet Street. On a happier occasion two years earlier, the cartoon on the right illustrated the menu for a special lunch given for Bob Findlay on the occasion of his eightieth birthday. Bob was John Morgan's predecessor as my Sports Editor, and his only bad friends were the gee-gees!

159

Telegraph boxing correspondent, delivered the address for Des, and he reminded us of how he had, with typical wit, nicknamed him 'Saunders of the Liver'. Apart from his friendship, I realised as I sat in St Bride's with my memories that I also had good reason to be thankful for Desmond's imagination. He used to hover over me when I was compiling my expenses after trips abroad, and he would insist on me bumping mine up so that his did not look too overcooked. *Never let facts spoil a good story!* I remember how in New York for one of the Patterson-Johansson fights four of us shared a huge hired Cadillac to go to and from the training camps. It was Des who used his charm on the hire car company receptionist to get her to run off four individual receipts. Naughty, yes, but massaging the expenses was considered a perk of the job.

Des once sent back a piece from Chicago (that I illustrated) in which he wrote in his graphic way about the old gangsters, and of how he had witnessed the place where Legs Diamond had been gunned down and where the blood was still wet on the pavement. His imagination had run riot, and I did not help with drawings of the Chicago inhabitants looking like Al Capone clones. When the story appeared in the *Express* the article was reprinted in Chicago, and Des and I were held up to ridicule by the local press and dignitaries who were trying to rid Chicago of the gangster image. Yes, Des, you old rascal, never let facts spoil a good story.

It was at one of the memorial services at St Bride's that I last had a reunion with another valued Fleet Street friend, Ian Wooldridge, who continues to decorate the *Daily Mail* with his beautifully written prose. He is from the old school who will know that I am speaking the truth when I say the 'good old days' will never be repeated. Seeing Ian reminded me of a golf tournament in which he played a round with *Express* cricket writers Crawford White and Keith 'The Wizard of Oz' Miller and myself. Off one particular tee, Ian – who has a peculiar low-down grip as if he is strangling a turkey – put two successive balls out of bounds. Then Keith Miller sliced two off course. Crawford went off somewhere into the rough, and I managed to get on to the fairway but hardly any distance at all. Watching all this with a mixture of lofty disdain and quiet amusement was Ted Dexter, who was in the four held up behind us. He just happened to be one of the finest cricketer-golfers ever to hold bat and club. As Nugget Miller put down a third ball, he said to Dexter, 'What d'you think I should take here, your Lordship?' Dexter appeared to give it some consideration, and then replied: 'How about the next train home?' For once in his life, Keith was lost for words. The imperious 'Lord' Ted later offered me a lift home in the private plane that he piloted. 'No thanks,' I told him. 'I never fly with amateurs.'

If I had a rival sports cartoonist, it was Ian Wooldridge's gifted *Daily Mail* colleague William Jones, who drew under the pen name of Jon. He was a Welsh Army captain who became famous during the war for his Two Types cartoon

"NOW LISTEN, AND YOU'LL FIND OUT WHY HE IS THE FUNNIEST COMEDIAN IN THE WORLD."

series in the *Union Jack*, featuring the adventures of a couple of comical and at times cynical British soldiers. We met up on the *Sunday Pictorial* after the war, and he moved on with great success to the *News Chronicle* and then to the *Daily Mail*. Jon was a charmer, who had the gift of getting his cartoon point across simply and often with a hidden bite to give an edge to the humour. This proud and talented man, who had served his country in the North African campaign, died in sad circumstances not long after being mugged in the middle of London. What a way to treat a hero.

On the few times that I venture back to my old haunts you can almost hear the ghosts of Fleet Street's past wailing at the passing of a way of life that made the Street the most exciting and, quite literally, most intoxicating place on earth. The thunder of rolling presses has given way to the chatter of office clerks and secretaries, and you can now cross Fleet Street comfortably without risk of being knocked down by evening newspaper vans racing each other to get the latest editions on the streets. They could have given lessons to Michael Schumacher in to how to knock a rival out of the way. Where have they all gone? My guess is that they have become London cabbies.

Even sadder is the disappearance of a whole family of printers – type-setters, compositors, machine minders and hot metal workers. They have been wiped out by a bloody revolution that has taken the newspaper industry kicking and screaming into a new era. It seems to me that the business is now run by bookkeepers. They dictate the terms of newspaper production rather than the editors, who have become puppets of accountants more concerned with balance sheets than broadsheets (and, of course, tabloids). I know that balancing the books is all very necessary, but a lot of the fun has been squeezed out of the newspaper game. And that's what it was in my peak years in the Street: a game.

I knew I had 'arrived' as an accepted member of the Street elite when, soon after joining the *Express*, I was asked for a self caricature for hanging on the

wall of The Devereaux, a quaint old pub tucked away in a courtyard opposite the Law Courts where Fleet Street meets The Strand. I looked out proudly from a collection of Fleet Street's finest, sharing the wall with an array of barristers and judges from across the road. We called it the Rogues' Gallery. Other favourite watering holes at that end of the Street were The George and The Wig and Pen, where I still hold membership. On a walk down memory lane (it sometimes used to be a stagger), I called in at The Devereaux to toast my portrait. Like all my old printer pals, van drivers and hot metal workers, I had vanished. 'Oh, we've recently been refurbished,' an Irish barman told me. 'Dose old pictures were considered not suitable with the new image.' Not suitable. Now there's an epitaph. Roy Ullyett does not live here any more. He's not suitable.

As I get older, I find my mind escaping more and more into the past. It's nice and comfortable there. If I close my eyes, I can see myself walking into the marbled magnificence of the *Express* lobby in the days before they put up huge ugly glass petitions as security. On my memory screen I banter with the reception staff and the one-legged lift man, a war hero. 'Going up,' I say to him. 'Everything's going up.' He rewards me with a sunny smile, sets course for the second floor and asks what tomorrow's cartoon will be about. 'That will be telling,' I say, hiding the fact that I do not have a clue. I will have day-dreamed my way to the office. My first port of call will be the sports desk where chummy

CHEER UP COBBER! YOU MUST HAVE ENJOYED THEIR SINGING.

statistics man Harry Cook, who used to work on Beaverbrook's house staff, will feed me all the tape messages from the various agencies. John 'The Welsh' Lloyd, a legendary sub-editor famous for allowing half of Wales to lodge with him at his Gray's Inn Road apartment, will try to talk me into drawing a cartoon about Harry Secombe, Tom Jones and Max Boyce in a scrum with Joe Erskine, Gareth Edwards, Barry John and John Charles. I am rescued by sports department secretary Cora Weston telling John that Shirley Bassey wants him on the telephone (I dedicate the above cartoon to generous John the Welsh, with thanks for the many favours he did me and all our old *Express* colleagues).

I read through the agency tapes, and then sound out deputy sports editor Norman Dixon with an idea. Norman is a bubbling, inspirational character from Barrow-in-Furness who counts every day as a bonus. In his wallet, he carries a scribbled note that was left with him by his major when Norman lay badly wounded in a field in France during the war. It is an apology for having to leave him behind. He had been left to die, but he dragged himself off into a hiding place and survived to tell the tale. Norman kindly chuckles at my verbal joke that I will

163

attempt to turn into an illustration for the next morning's paper. I remember to give my imaginative expense sheet to wonderfully organized sports editor's secretary Doris Bishop before wandering off to one of half a dozen offices that I have shared for more than forty years with Michael Cummings. We call it The Cell. There is hardly room to swing Sylvester the Cat, and Michael and I nod to each other from behind our back-to-back drawing boards. He is deep in thought on how best to make a telling political point, and is producing a drawing fit to hang in the Tate Gallery. Before being shut in The Cell with Cummings, I had wandered around the Black Lubianka like a lost soul. They just could not find any office space for me, and I was given a temporary 'home' by (Harry) Chapman Pincher, without question the greatest investigative reporter in Fleet Street history. He had an incredible range of contacts, and was always taking coded messages from Whitehall sources. Every day there was a Deep Throat on the telephone telling him government secrets. I don't know if I was considered a security risk, but it was decided that I should be housed with another cartoonist rather than the man with the inside line to Downing Street. Cummings and Ullyett were teamed like a pair of full backs.

For a cartoonist, Cummings was a very serious-minded bloke. We had about as much in common as Karl Marx and Groucho Marx. I'll give you two guesses which of us represented Groucho (Clue: I had an ever-present pipe rather than a cigar). Michael thought of Ramsey as a former Archbishop of Canterbury, while you can put my knowledge of politics in a gnat's knapsack and still have room for a sandwich. But we suffered, and often enjoyed, each other's company, and when we had exhausted the few subjects we had in common we would take refuge behind our boards and get on with our drawing, Michael lampooning politicians and me looking for laughs in the world of sport. Our little office was sound-proofed following protests from Michael about the shrill, parrot-like noise of columnist Eve Perrick's voice in an adjoining office. 'How can a man concentrate with that racket going on?' Michael complained. 'That voice makes me want to do something nasty with my pencil!' They spent a lot of time and money putting sound proofing around the office walls, and the day after the work was finished Ms 'Parrot' Perrick was moved to another part of the building. On reflection, the sound proofing would have been better placed in Chapman Pincher's room of national secrets.

Lord Beaverbrook

Cummings, a Lord Beaverbrook 'discovery', was steeped in Fleet Street history. His father, A.J. Cummings, was the political editor of the *News Chronicle* and his mother a distinguished artist. He started on the left wing *Tribune*, which was about as far removed from the *Express* doctrine as you can get. But he was a closet right winger, and wrote to Lord Beaverbrook just before the war offering his services. Michael showed me the Beaver's handwritten reply that he had kept. 'Dear Mr Cummings,' Beaverbrook wrote from the South of France. 'I have arranged for you to meet Mr Christiansen. I am just an old gentleman who wants to sit in the sun.' Within months of writing that letter, Beaver was sitting in Churchill's wartime cabinet as the minister for aircraft production, and Cummings was on the *Express* staff at the start of a career in which he was to become a legend in both Fleet Street and Westminster.

Cummings and I were always getting requests for originals. I was only too happy to let mine go, but Michael had a strict policy that he had to be paid for them. He used to put enormous concentration and effort into each cartoon, and did not feel inclined to let them go for nothing. I recall him falling out with Tony Benn, who wanted three cartoons but apparently refused to pay, so Michael declined to let him have them.

Sadly, Michael passed on to the great art room in the sky in October 1997, forty-five years after we first shared an office. We did not have a cross word in all the time we spent together, which speaks volumes for his patience with my pipe! There were few to touch him for making biting political comment with a pen and a diligently constructed drawing. His pen was definitely mightier than a sword. Rest easy, old friend. Back to my memory screen. I stare at the blank sheet on the drawing board, and then start to lightly pencil in the idea that is sitting in embryo form at the back of my brain. Once I am happy with the general outline, I then concentrate on capturing the look of my 'victim'. Often this comes immediately, perhaps with the help of a photograph. There are other times when I cannot get close to it, and decide on a different subject. When I am satisfied, I ink over the pencil lines with a paintbrush that I use like a pen. I have a gallery of regular visitors to my cartoons. My favourite, along with my goalkeeper, is the 'MCC type', a retired colonel who I call on any time that I want to poke some fun at the creaking sports establishment. My work can take anything from twenty minutes to two hours, depending on the detail required and the degree of difficulty of the subject.

The MCC type

Then comes the important decision of the day. Where to lunch? Do I fancy roast beef at the Albion, Dover sole at the Cheshire Cheese, steak and kidney pud and a game of snooker at the Press Club, a pie and a pint with the lads in the City Golf Club, or a liquid lunch at El Vino's? I can taste the food as I think back on those lovely times that are lost and gone forever. Returning to the office after lunch I would invariably have to draw a new cartoon to reflect a breaking news story. Sometimes the half bottle of Beaujolais I had consumed would inspire me to have a little private joke within the joke of the cartoon.

It was a trade secret that the mischievous Carl Giles used to slip hidden jokes into his cartoons, usually of the rude variety. A famous one was when he had a line of RAF recruits eyeing a Sophia Loren look-alike, and he drew bumps in the groin areas of the soldiers. It was spotted, and he was forced to air-brush the bumps out. But he got away with a lot of little gems. In the background of the cartoon he drew to mark my twenty-one years with the Express he managed to make two golf balls look like testicles. I did not go down the rude road, but my

little 'in' joke would be to drop personal friends into anonymous roles in my cartoons. For instance, the club chairman in the cartoon on this page is, in fact, a likeness of one of my closest pals, Nelson Mitchell, who was for several years chairman of Southend United Football Club. I would also sketch my Southend boxing promoter chum, Johnny Levine, into background scenes. And, like Alfred Hitchcock making a fleeting appearance in his films, I would often draw myself into a cartoon.

It was all harmless fun and helped make the afternoon tick by after a pleasant lunch. Ah, what lovely days.

Back in the present, I find I now start each day by reading the obituary page, and if my name is not on it I get up (that's a joke borrowed from my old golfing buddy Bob Hope).

Maggie and I have joined that peculiar species: New Age Golden Oldies. Many of us are living longer now, and there are enough of us senior citizens to have a lot of muscle in the political world. When I've got the time I am going to organise a movement called GOAL ... the Golden Oldies Action League. Our objective will be to bring back some of the old standards and principles that we oldies know would be good for the country. The thing that appears to be disappearing from society is respect and courtesy.

Our home in Westcliff looks out across the Thames Estuary, and over the local cenotaph remembering those who gave their lives in two daft world wars. The gleaming white monument stands behind a square grass lawn on which is carved out in huge white lettering the message, 'Lest We Forget'. Local teenagers have taken to using the steps of the cenotaph and the grass lawn for skate-boarding stunts. When I shout at them to go away, they reply with language that would make Fred Trueman blush. They need to be taught respect.

The over-paid and over-indulged footballers who we see on our television screens screaming insults at the referees need to be taught respect. So, too, do the tennis players who verbally abuse umpires, the batsmen who refuse to walk, the rugby players who stamp on opponents. I could go on, but I feel I am boring you. I shall get off my soapbox having, I hope, made my point that what we need back in our lives is good old-fashioned respect, and reverence where it is due. That should be our GOAL.

The eighties and nineties have merged and blurred into each other in my overloaded memory. Under the friendly and creative guidance of my fifth sports editor, David Emery, I continued to cartoon for the *Express* up until 1997, which meant that I had been a Fleet Street scribbler for the little matter of sixty-four years (they could take the man out of Fleet Street, but they could never take Fleet Street out of the man).

I was reduced to pocket-sized cartoons in the new tabloid format, but any cartoonist worth his salt and vinegar should be able to raise at least a smile even if he is working on a postage stamp. There were plenty of great characters to keep me in business on my last lap, none more entertaining and at the same time aggravating than John McEnroe. Listening to him now as an observant and authoritative television expert, it is hard to realise that this is the same person who just a blink of an eye ago was such a temperamental and uncouth brat on the court. He surpassed himself on his way to defeat by the gentlemanly Stefan Edberg in the 1992 Wimbledon championships. I could not believe my eyes and ears as he swore at a linesman six times in ten seconds, an outburst that was picked up by an ITN microphone. This is a censored version of what shocked millions of TV viewers heard: 'Blank, you stupid blanker. Good blanking call, you son of a blanking bitch.' It cost McEnroe a maximum $10,000 fine, which worked out at $1,000 a second.

The major change I have seen in sport is the way money has become the god. Footballers earned a maximum eight pounds a week when Alex James first took me under his wing back in the mid-1930s. Now one player in the Premiership earns in one week what the entire Arsenal first-team squad earned between them in a season. Sounds crazy, but it's true.

The British Open champion today collects a cheque for something in the region of £150,000, plus ten times more in sponsorship and endorsement deals. I was talking to Arthur Havers at Lytham back in the 1960s when a young lad came up and asked for my autograph. 'Wouldn't you prefer the autograph of an Open champion?' I said, indicating Arthur. The lad thought I was pulling his leg, not realising that Havers had won the Open in 1923 when he beat the immortal Walter Hagen by one stroke at Troon. His prize money was £100, plus a gold medal. Arthur spent the hundred pounds furnishing and decorating his bungalow, and put his framed medal on the wall in pride of place. Thieves broke into the bungalow and stole the medal. It can be a cruel world.

My fiftieth year in Fleet Street [not counting Hitler's rude interruption] was marked with a pleasant missive from a bod at the Palace asking if I would be willing to accept an OBE from Her Majesty the Queen. I am a dyed-in-the-blue Royalist, and was greatly honoured. Maggie and I went off to Buck House to collect the gong, and who should be included in the same honours list but one of my favourite targets of all, Frederick Sewards Trueman. Fred, bless him, reckoned that he should have collected my award as well as his own for all the material he had provided me with over the years. He has grabbed most of the originals ['I bloody earned em,' he says, with that Desperate Dan grimace of his].

Thank you Fred, Sir Alf, Muhammad, Cloughie, Sir Colin, Sir Stanley, Sir Gordon, Sir Matt, nobbly Nobby, wee Alex James, Compo, Bud, Monsewer Eddie Gray, Eric Morecambe, Harry 'The Nose' Levene, Jack 'King' Solomons, Our 'Enery, Sir Bobby, Mooro, Big Jack, Barnacle, Sir Don, Sir Len, Sir Jack, Olly Milburn, Greavsie, Denis the Menace, SuperMex, Jacko, Golden Bear, Peerless Fred Perry, Untouchable Henry Cotton, Brown Bomber, Sullen Sonny, Freud Floyd, Ingo, Fearless Freddie Mills, Bruce Woodcock, Randy, Sugar Ray, Lillee and Thomson, Mary Rand, Ginny Wade, Billie-Jean, Christine, Illy, Dickie Bird, Boris, Boycs, Both, Superbrat, and all the Rats ... and the whole army of sports and show business personalities who became my pen friends. What would I have done without you all? Thank you from the bottom of my inkwell.

Now, before going to gather lilacs with my darling Maggie, I leave you with a last taste of my work in the closing spell of my sixty-plus years of drawing a wage in Fleet Street. I loved every second of it. Would that I could do it all again.

WHO HAS THE FILTHIEST MOUTH?

(A) McENROE (B) CONNORS

(C) BABY EATING HIS CHRISTMAS DINNER

"NEW BALLS PLEASE, AND A FRESH MOUTH-WASH FOR MR McENROE"

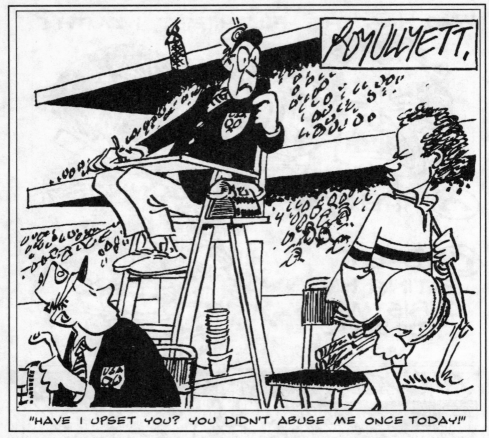

"HAVE I UPSET YOU? YOU DIDN'T ABUSE ME ONCE TODAY!"

"WITH THE MONEY YOU EARN, MR McENROE, I WOULD HAVE THOUGHT YOU COULD AFFORD A BABY-SITTER."

"HAVE A NICE FLIGHT, MR CONNORS, AND PLEASE TRY NOT TO ABUSE THE PILOT. HE WILL TELL YOU TO GET NETTED."

FIRST THE BAD NEWS: BOYCOTT IS OUT

SECOND THE WORSE NEWS: MCENROE IS IN!

WHO'S THE OTHER BEARDED CHAP NEXT TO BOYCOTT?

"I THINK THIS COULD COST ENGLAND THE GILLETTE RAZOR SPONSORSHIP"

"I DIDN"T VOTE FOR WOMEN JOINING THE MCC. I CAN'T REMEMBER WHAT THEY ARE!"

"THE NEXT TIME YOU POKE A PAKISTANI UMPIRE WITH YOUR FINGER, MAKE SURE YOU KEEP IT STRAIGHT AS IN THE MCC COACHING MANUAL!"

"HOW ABOUT THAT FOR AN INDIAN ROPE TRICK!"

"DICKIE'S WELL PREPARED IF THERE'S ANOTHER BOMB SCARE. THAT'S A SNIFFER DOG."

"I THOUGHT YOU SAID AN MBE WOULD NOT GO TO YOUR HEAD!"

"OUR NEXT STEP TOWARDS WORLD PEACE IS TO STOP ENGLAND AND PAKISTAN PLAYING TEST MATCHES!"

CHATTERBOX PRINCESS ANNE DISTRACTS TORVILL AND DEAN RIVALS

"PERHAPS WE SHOULD SEND HER DOWN UNDER WITH ENGLAND TO HELP DISTRACT THE AUSSIE CRICKETERS."

FYLDE R.F.C.

FYLDE

ORRELL

PTS

"IT'S GOING TO TAKE ME TIME TO GET USED TO RETIREMENT. I PUT THIS ON BY FORCE OF HABIT."

"I'VE COME PREPARED IN CASE ERICA ROE DOES ANOTHER STREAK."

"THIS IS RIDICULOUS, STEVE. WITH THE MONEY WE'RE EARNING WHY DON'T WE CALL A CAB?"

"RIGHT, SEB, I'M HANGING ON TIGHT. LET'S GO ALL OUT FOR GOLD, SILVER AND BRONZE."

179

"DO YOU HOPE TO THROW YOUR RACKET AS FAR AS THOMPSON HURLS HIS JAVELIN?"

"VE MUST HAF VAYS OF MAKING BECKER STOP TALKING!"

"WELL, GINNY, THIS IS WHAT WE CALL IN THE RACING WORLD 'WADE IN!'"

JACK CHARLTON INTRODUCES HIS EASY-
AS-ABC COACHING SCHEME FOR THE
PARENTS OF FOOTBALL HOOLIGANS

"WE'VE GOT THE BEST
SEAT AT WEMBLEY TO
SEE ELTON'S HAIR WHEN
HE TAKES HIS HAT OFF
FOR THE NATIONAL
ANTHEM."

"ALL RIGHT LADS. WE'RE
NOT GOING TO LET A FEW
INJURIES STAND BETWEEN
US AND GLORY. ENGLAND
EXPECTS ..."

"THE REFEREE WANTS NO RISK OF ANY FURTHER TROUBLE WITH HIGGINS LEAVING THE TABLE DURING A MATCH!"

"VERY INTERESTING, BUT I'M TELLING YOU THE FORECAST WAS FOR FREEZING WEATHER AT WEMBLEY FOR THE FOOTBALL, NOT THE SNOOKER."

"CLEAN THE BALL BECAUSE IT JUMPED! IT'S JUST AS WELL YOU'RE NOT PLAYING FOR THE ENGLAND CRICKET TEAM IN THE WEST INDIES!"

"CLOUGHIE? IAN BOTHAM HERE. NOW TELL ME AGAIN ... HOW DO I BEGIN TO WALK ON WATER?"

"WITH ALL THIS TALK OF BUNGS, IT LOOKS AS IF CLOUGHIE'S FORGOTTEN HOW TO WALK ON WATER."

"DOES IT NOT STRIKE YOU FUNNY, SENORS, THAT THEY STILL CALL IT THE US MASTERS?"

"IWELL, DOCTOR, HE WAS TRYING OUT HIS SAM TORRANCE BROOM-HANDLE PUTTER AND THIS IS THE RESULT."

"IN SEVVY'S COACHING BOOK, IT SAYS ALL YOU HAVE TO DO IS TAKE AN EIGHT-IRON AND PUT THE BALL AND THE TREE ON TO THE GREEN."

"CAN I HAVE YOUR AUTOGRAPH, PLEASE MR NICKLAUS. I LOST THE ONE YOU GAVE ME WHEN I WAS A LAD."

"I'M AFRAID IT'S TIME ROY PACKED UP. THE OLD BOY'S MEMORY HAS GONE."

"YOU'VE FORGOTTEN TO ASK DEVON MALCOLM TO SHOW HIS APPRECIATION!"

"CONGRATULATIONS, GAZZA. IT WAS A PLEASURE NOT HAVING TO WATCH YOU PLAY. I MUST THANK GRAHAM TAYLOR FOR THE BEST NON-SELECTION OF HIS INTERNATIONAL CAREER."

"GREAT! MY FIRST CHANCE TO GET A RED CARD IN AN INTERNATIONAL MATCH."

THAT'S ALL FROM ROY.
NOW HIS FRIENDS AND
'VICTIMS' TAKE OVER ...

THIS is a fairly unique chapter in as much as the book's author knows nothing about it! Roy will not realise until he opens the book that I have rummaged through his old correspondence files, cuttings books and archival material and have surreptitiously raided his memory to find out just what his 'victims' thought of his cartoon capers.

I first put the idea of this book to Roy in 1966 when we were team-mates in the *Daily Express* sports department. He thought it was such a splendid project that we took just thirty-two years to get into print. Roy thoughtfully acknowledged my suggestion with the cartoon note reproduced here on the left. Ever since, I have had a complex about my nose. Thanks, Roy.

Roy Ullyett lives up to everything you would expect in a sports cartoonist. He looks as if he has clambered out of one of his cartoons, and is like a walking, talking caricature, taking a light-hearted and occasionally waspish look at the sports world over the hedge that is his trademark ginger handlebar moustache. There is a permanent twinkle in his eyes, and the hint of a smile playing at the corner of the lips which are invariably curled round his favourite S-shape Sherlock Holmes pipe. You will

To Norman with thanks and a lot of affection. You'll never make a good ghost — you carry too much weight!

Roy Ullyett '66.

find nothing in the least false or affected about Roy. He is an authentic, gold-plated English eccentric, slightly dotty, a little naive and totally genuine. It would be easy to mistake him for a member of the aristocracy, with his Harold Macmillan eyelids, slightly hooked nose, immaculately tailored suits, and his tall, upright guardsman-like bearing. This is why it was so easy for Desmond Hackett to travel the world with him calling him 'my Lord' and getting all the perks that come with that station in life. You can heat your hands on the warmth that generates from him. He truly is one of nature's gentlemen; an amiable assassin, who pokes gentle fun at his 'victims' without ever crossing the fine line between humour and humiliation. There is not a cruel bone in Roy's body.

I have known (and adored) Roy since first meeting him in the late 1950s when I was a reporter on *Boxing News*, the trade paper of the fight game. I stood alongside him at the back of the Thomas A'Beckett gymnasium in Bermondsey as he sketched young Henry Cooper going through a training session. His pencil skipped lightly over the sketchpad in what at first seemed unintelligible squiggles, but within moments Our 'Enery had been transferred from the punchbag to the page. My first impression, that this was a magician at work, has never left me. He is a true master of his art (pun intended). You could never teach anybody to draw the Ullyett way. His style is as unique as a Picasso. Nobody can capture sports competitors in the same way as Roy. He can make them outrageously aggressive (see Fred Trueman, page 93), desperately manic (Dennis Lillee,132), hilariously comical (Nobby Stiles, 146), quietly proud (Bobby Moore,101), and he can be tear-jerkingly moving (Munich 1958, 69).

With just a few flourishes on his sketchpad from his lightning-fast pen, he can reduce a serious moment in sport to a classic of comedy. If anybody should have an art gallery exhibition it is Roy Ullyett. He is, putting it simply but accurately, a genius of an artist. E.M. Wellings, distinguished former cricket correspondent of the London *Evening News*, once wrote: 'Roy Ullyett is the most accomplished sports cartoonist in the world.' Typically, Roy chuckles at the description. 'I never did get round to paying him for that,' he says.

Roy's next boastful remark will be his first, and the hardest thing in helping him to compile his memoirs was to get him to talk about himself. I considered it a privilege just to watch him work. When facing his drawing board and a virgin sheet of paper, he goes off into a half trance, his friendly eyes narrow and suddenly his huge right hand that would not look out of place on a heavyweight boxer starts moving as if with a mind of its own. Suddenly that heavyweight fist is as light and delicate as a lilac in springtime as his pencil dances across the page to a tune that only Roy can hear. The first few lines make no sense at all, and then from out of a maze of scribbles a face appears. The limbs follow, inevitably with the nobbly knees and elbows that are an Ullyett copyright. In no time at all – just minutes – he has the outline of his cartoon. He then closes his right eye while focusing on the main character, and concentrates hard while bringing the identikit he has in his mind to the page. Nine times out of ten, he is spot on with the likeness at the first time of drawing. Next it is his narrow brush, dipped in coal-black ink, that he flourishes over the pencilled lines.

Roy is his own judge and jury until he has finished the cartoon. Then he looks for confirmation that what he has drawn is one, funny, and two, accurate. Steve Curry, who followed me as chief football writer for the *Express*, is one of Fleet Street's finest joke tellers. Roy would push the cartoon under his nose and gauge his reaction. Steve would always laugh, and Roy would shuffle away to get the next opinion. Once he had satisfied himself that there was unanimous approval, he would submit his cartoon and then take Des Hackett off for a deserved drink or three.

'I can remember and tell a joke,' said Steve Curry. 'But these are stories that have been thought up by others. Every day Roy comes up with something original and usually very funny, unless he is trying to make a serious point and then he can use his pen like a rapier. The man is a genius, and bloody nice with it. I would say he's the most popular person I have come across in our business. Nobody but nobody has a bad word to say about Roy.'

Age is now just beginning to weary him, and the famous ginger moustache is starting to grey and droop, but Roy still continues to draw for his favourite charity organisations, for whom he has raised thousands and thousands of pounds. He has lost none of his talent to amuse.

We are coming to you late in what 84-years-young Roy insists on calling 'a funny life, so far.' He and his adorable and adoring wife, Maggie, sit looking out for hours from their Westcliff-on-Sea apartment balcony towards the Thames Estuary, sharing more than fifty years of memories. Their daughter, Freya, son-in-law John and grandchildren, Kate and Ben, drop in at regular intervals to add family warmth to the contented scene.

I have been privileged to share in their world, and to listen to Roy recalling his life and times. There is still, thankfully, some lead left in his pencil. And it *has* been quite a funny life, so far – as the following parade of witnesses are about to confirm ...

Note: The following quotes have been adapted from correspondence, cuttings, archival material and, occasionally, Roy's memory. If anybody wishes to sue, we will laugh them out of court.

PRINCE PHILIP, The Duke of Edinburgh (1976)

Roy Ullyett and I have been fellow Rats for many years, and I am happy to possess some of his cartoon originals. His cartoons not only make people laugh but invariably do some good, because many of them are auctioned for charitable causes. All his efforts on behalf of the Rats are greatly appreciated.

[Prince Philip was speaking on the occasion of Roy's 21st year as a Rat. He has now been a Rat for 42 years]

JACK SOLOMONS (1961)

Roy is not only a great cartoonist, but also a great artist. There is nobody to touch him for capturing fight action on paper. His drawings of the world champions are in great demand because they are so amazingly accurate. He has illustrated my boxing programmes for many years, and each one of them becomes a collectors' item because of his contribution. My office walls are decorated with Ullyett originals. They are real works of art.

FRED TRUEMAN (1972)

If Roy wasn't such a smashing bloke, I'd punch him on the nose for the way he has portrayed me over the years. If it weren't for me, I think his pencil would have dried up long ago. Seriously though, I am honoured to have had him draw me so often and his originals are treasured. His marvellous eye for the funny side of sport has given us all a good laugh for many a year, and it must be very rewarding for him to know that his cartoons have made thousands of pounds for charity.

SIR STANLEY MATTHEWS (1980)

I considered it a privilege to have Roy draw me during my playing days. I used to contact him for the originals when I was playing for Stoke and Blackpool because his cartoons were so marvellous. Sport is an all too serious business, and it's good to have somebody like Roy around to remind us of the funny side of things. He has a wonderful gift for drawing, and he has used it to give a lot of people a lot of pleasure.

BUD FLANAGAN (1966)

I have known Roy since his hedge of a moustache was just a little caterpillar. He is an absolute genius with that pen of his, and I cannot thank him enough for all that he has done to help me raise a lot of cash for many good causes including my Leukaemia Fund. He has been drawing me and my Crazy Gang buddies for so long that he has become crazy himself. His mad cartoons prove it. He is a very funny and a very lovely man.

HENRY COTTON (1974)

Roy and I have had a friendship going back more than thirty years. We have collaborated on golfing books together, and I am in awe of his talent. I like to think I can paint a bit, but when I see Roy's work I realise that I am just a novice. He could be an outstanding landscape artist if he put his mind to it, but he prefers to specialise in cartooning and making us all laugh. For that, we should be grateful. There is not another like him. He is one of the great characters of Fleet Street.

MUHAMMAD ALI (1976)

I like your drawings, and I like your style, but you don't pay me, so you won't see me for a while. Seriously, Roy is an unforgettable character, and a wonderful ambassador for England. Whenever I see him I start to smile. He makes me feel good just being in his company. I like to tug on that mustash of his, and pretend that it's false. Roy has been ringside at my fights since I was an amateur in the Rome Olympics. I like him a lot, and I just love those cartoons of his.

ALAN FREEMAN (1987)

Roy did me the honour of presenting me with a framed drawing of myself when I was King Rat. It has pride of place on my wall. What talent the man has! Roy is legendary in the Grand Order of Water Rats because of the great work he does for them year in and year out. He has given so much fun and pleasure to so many people during his life, both as a cartoonist and as a human being. We are proud to have him as a Rat.

TONY JACKLIN (1982)

Roy and I have had great fun together over the years. He has been capturing my adventures on the golf course since I was just a rookie. It's important to have somebody like Roy around to gently remind us that golf – all sport, for that matter – is just a game. When you are starting to take it too seriously, just have a loook at an Ullyett cartoon. It will quickly put things in perspective, and give you a good laugh.

SIR LEN HUTTON (1969)

I knew I had arrived as a cricketer when Roy started to feature me in his cartoons. He used to have great fun with my nose, and made it look as if it had been broken by Joe Louis. He was at The Oval the day I completed my record innings of 364 runs in 1938, and I treasured the cartoon that he drew showing me up there with the greats of the game. I took my cricket perhaps a little too seriously, and it was always refreshing to turn to Roy for a smile.

BOB HOPE (1980)

I can remember meeting Roy for the first time in the 1940s. You don't forget it because he has such an unforgettable face. I think he stole that moustache of his from Aintree. It used to be one of the Grand National jumps. We've had a lot of fun together on the golf course, and his cartoons have helped me in my fund-raising events over in Britain. Whenever he draws me he makes my nose seem like a ski run. I admire his talent, but – let's face it – he does not quite capture my classic looks.

BOBBY CHARLTON (1974)

Roy was quite a favourite in the Manchester United dressing-room in my playing days. He was always featuring somebody from the team and giving us a good laugh. We particularly liked his gormless goalkeeper and the other members of his barmy side, and we used to try to spot the players he had based them on. Sir Matt was a great fan of Roy's, and he took great delight in seeing Nobby and the rest of us sent up by his pencil.

SIR MATT BUSBY (1969)

Roy is a loveable rascal! Whenever I am with him I feel as if I am in the company of a character from one of his cartoons. He has got a permanent twinkle in his eye, and that moustache of his seems like a big grin on his face. I feel honoured every time he draws me. At least he is kind to me, unlike poor Nobby Stiles who has taken some terrible stick because of Roy's portrayal of him. But we all accept that it is in good fun.

NOBBY STILES (1970)

The lads in the dressing-room are always teasing me over the way Roy draws me. He makes me seem like a character out of a comic. But I have learned to laugh at it, and I know that Roy means no malice. He teaches you to laugh at yourself, so that cannot be a bad thing. Let's face it, I'm not the best looking thing on two feet when I've got my teeth out. I must be a gift to Roy with his eye on the funny side of sport. It's good to have him looking at the lighter side of our tough game.

HARRY LEVENE (1975)

My old friend Roy has taken so many liberties with my nose that he's ruined my love life! Des Hackett once got me to pretend that I was going to sue Roy for 'facial assassination'. But, as Des said, they would have laughed me out of court. I look on Roy's constant attacks on my nose as a privilege. It is better than being ignored, and all publicity is good publicity. But I think he was taking it a bit far to compare my nose with Concorde's! Roy deserves a punch on the nose for that one!

TREVOR BROOKING (1996)

Roy drew a fantastic caricature of me to mark my year as captain of the Variety Club Golfing Society. He had a gag about me not being keen on heading a ball, and it gave me a lot of pleasure to be able to point out that I headed the goal that won the FA Cup for West Ham against Arsenal at Wembley in 1980. He is a master cartoonist and always goes out of his way to help the Variety Club with their charity work.

JOE DAVIS (1956)

I first met Roy in the early 1930s, and I remember being so impressed by his cartoon in the *Star* that I asked for the original. We have been good friends ever since, and he continues to make me laugh with his work in the *Express*. There is nobody to touch him in his field, and he is not only very funny but also uncannily accurate with the way he captures people. He is also a lovely man and very good company.

ARTHUR CHRISTIANSEN (1953)

We have signed the best sports cartoonist in the world. As editor of the *Express* I could not be happier. It completes the best team of cartoonists on any paper. There are thousands of people who draw, but there is only one Roy Ullyett. He has such a distinctive style, and can get across with a brilliant cartoon more than some writers can convey in five thousand words. I have also got myself a golf companion, and I hope he will help me get my handicap down as low as his.

SONNY LISTON (1963)

Roy Ullyett makes me laugh. I am not sure what he is saying half the time, but his drawings are very special. I have seen his portraits of old fighters like Joe Louis and Sugar Ray Robinson and can understand why he is so highly rated. He was at the ringside for both my fights with Floyd Patterson, and he has given me the drawings he did of Patterson going down. In return, I am going to give him an introduction to his cartoon annual. I'm not really into reading much, but I love his cartoons.

DANNY LA RUE (1986)

I have no hesitation in describing Roy as a genius. He is a truly great entertainer, who manages to make people laugh day in and day out with a cleverly created cartoon. He drew a magnificent cartoon to mark my year as the King Rat, and I was thrilled when he presented me with the framed original that is now on the wall at my home. To have an Ullyett cartoon is one of the perks we all look forward to as King Rat.

HENRY COOPER (1997)

Roy seems to have been around for ever. I can remember laughing at his cartoons when I was a kid, and felt proud when he started to feature me in his gallery. One of my favourite cartoons is one in which you see only my feet. I was lying in a hospital operating theatre and the surgeon was trying to remember whether he had to operate on my left hand or my right knee. Everybody loves Roy. What a great character!

JACK NICKLAUS (1982)

I look forward to seeing Roy whenever I come over for an event. He is the epitomy of the English gentleman, and that huge moustache of his gives so much character to his face. You have only got to look at him to know that this is a man who makes people smile for a living. His early cartoons of me made me look as huge as an elephant, and I used to think that maybe I should get around to shedding some pounds. Apart from being a fine artist, I respect him for his knowledge of golf.

ERIC MORECAMBE (1975)

When I first met Roy I thought that he had flown in without a plane. That moustache of his is so big that he has to carry a 'wide load' sign on his back. The hardest thing in the world is to make people laugh (ask Des O'Connor), but Roy manages to do it the hardest way by drawing on a sheet of paper. His illustrations for the column that I have in the *Express* are just brilliant. He is a born entertainer, and a fascinating person to meet. I hope he remembers to put the tash out every night.

FRED PERRY (1980)

My memories of Roy go to before I won the first of my Wimbledon titles. He was very keen on tennis, and because of his father's link with Slazengers he attended all the top tournaments. I used to see him sketching on the sidelines, and he never failed to amuse me with his early work in the *Star*. When he joined the *Express*, he got the national platform that he deserved, and now everybody knows what a class act he is.

This was drawn in 1966 when Henry Cooper underwent a cartilage operation

BILLY WRIGHT (1984)

I have always considered it an honour to have Roy drawing me for one of his cartoons. He has featured me many times since my days as a player with Wolves, and he has never failed to make me laugh – even when he was having digs at me when everything was going wrong for me during my last season as manager of Arsenal. I could never take offence at his cartoons because I knew it did me good to try to laugh at a crisis.

JACK DEMPSEY (1962)

Roy has given me a wonderful drawing of myself and the highlights of my career that will get a place of honour on the wall of my New York restaurant. I have had some good times with Roy and his colleague Desmond Hackett. They are splendid fellows to know, and whenever Roy comes into the restaurant we treat him like royalty. You get the impression that he was born in an English castle. He's certainly a king of cartoonists.

JACKIE STEWART (1973)

I have yet to forgive Roy for caricaturing me to look like Bugs Bunny! Seriously though, any famous sportsman in Britain knows he has not made it to the top until he has been 'done' by Roy. I have been with him on the golf course, and as he stands over six feet and has that huge fungus protuding beyond his ears you can never miss him, even when he's deep in the rough. I've been a fan of his since when he first started drawing in the Scottish *Daily Express*, and I am delighted that he has included me among his list of victims.

DAVID COLEMAN (1971)

No British journalist has provided more pleasure over the years than Roy Ullyett. He manages to make fun of sports competitors and officials without giving offence, and he meets the daily challenge of making readers smile with fresh and topical material. His humour is as kind as the man himself. I do not know anybody who does not like Roy, even those whom he has poked fun at with his pen. He does not laugh at them, but with them.

TREVOR BAILEY (1982)

Roy has literally known me all my life. We are near neighbours and even closer friends, but that has not meant he has spared me over the years. More than anybody else, Roy is responsible for my nickname, Barnacle, sticking to me. It just shows the power of his pen. He is the complete master of sports cartooning, but, much more important, he is an absolutely delightful chap. It has been a joy to know him.

JIMMY GREAVES (1997)

For as long as I can remember, Roy has been around with his pencil proving that football truly is a funny old game. I would liked to have seen Roy employed as the Minister for Sport. He would have put the fun back into all games. One of my best old pals, Norman 'Speedy' Quicke, was a photographer on the *Express*, and through him I got to know Roy well. He is just like a character out of his cartoons, and enormously likeable.

JOHN CONTEH (1985)

Roy's cartoons of me when I was on the way to the world championship were just unbelieveable. What a magic pencil he's got. He captured the action better than any photographer. I don't know anybody who objects to Roy drawing them, even when he is taking the mickey in his own special way. It's an honour to appear in an Ullyett cartoon, and I used to be delighted to see him coming to the gymnasium to work on preview material. He was like a breath of fresh air, and I could not wait to see what that all-seeing eye of his had picked up.

DESMOND HACKETT (1973)

Roy and I travelled the world together, and no man could have asked for a better companion. He looks like a lord and we lived like lords, and so I thought it fitting to introduce him to people as Lord Ullyett. The title suited him perfectly. While I was writing my reports, Roy would get that demon pencil to work and come up with a cartoon that said all that I had been trying to say in a thousand words. He is The Master.

Index

Page numbers in bold italics refer to illustrations